Windward
— BY KNIT PICKS —

Copyright 2018 © Knit Picks

All rights reserved. This book or any portion thereof may not be reproduced or used in any manner whatsoever without the express written permission of the publisher except for the use of brief quotations in a book review.

Photography by Amy Setter

Printed in the United States of America

First Printing, 2018

ISBN 978-1-62767-179-8

Versa Press, Inc
800-447-7829

www.versapress.com

CONTENTS

Julie's Sweater — 8

Straight & Arrow Cardigan — 16

Copan Hat — 24

Carrick Shawl — 28

Sestina Pullover — 32

MacAskill Scarf — 40

Diamond Lattice Pullover — 46

Wrought Iron Wrap — 52

Sionann Cardi — 58

Snohomish Pullover — 76

Torque Poncho — 82

Arisaig — 90

Dun Laoghaire — 98

Gren Stole — 106

Studio Cardi — 112

Piney Tweed Hat — 128

ALONG THE GALE-SCOURED SHORES OF THE OUTER HEBRIDES OR IN BLUSTERY URBAN CANYONS, CABLING PROVIDES THAT EXTRA PROTECTION YOU NEED WHEN YOU'RE HEADED INTO THE WIND. THESE PATTERNS ARE AS FAR FROM THE ARAN PULLOVER AS THAT "TRADITIONAL" SWEATER IS BEYOND THE FUNCTIONAL GANSEYS IT EVOLVED FROM, BUT THEY ALL PARTICIPATE IN THE SAME CRAFT LINEAGE.

PART OF THE APPEAL OF KNITTING IS THAT FORM AND FUNCTION COME TOGETHER SO SEAMLESSLY, AND CABLES ARE THE PERFECT BLEND OF SUBSTANCE AND STYLE. BRAIDED, WANDERING CABLES MAY HAVE STARTED OUT AS A WAY TO FORTIFY A SWEATER FOR THE RIGORS OF THE SEA, BUT NO CRAFTER, EVEN CENTURIES PAST, WORKS ONLY TO THE SATISFACTION OF PRACTICALITY AND THERE CONSIDERS HER WORK DONE. THE PATTERNS WE'VE GATHERED HERE ARE ONLY THE LATEST RESULTS OF THAT UNIVERSAL COMPULSION NOT JUST TO OPTIMIZE, BUT ALSO BEAUTIFY.

JULIE'S SWEATER

by Kristen TenDyke

FINISHED MEASUREMENTS
31 (35, 39, 43, 47, 51, 55, 59, 63)" finished bust measurement; garment is meant to be worn with 1–3" of positive ease

YARN
Knit Picks Wool of the Andes Worsted (100% Peruvian Highland Wool; 110 yards/50g): Cobblestone Heather 24283, 11 (12, 12, 14, 14, 15, 16, 17, 18) balls

NEEDLES
US 7 (4.5mm) DPNs and 16" and 32" circular needles, or size to obtain gauge

NOTIONS
Yarn Needle, Stitch Markers, Cable Needle, Scrap yarn or stitch holders

GAUGE
16 sts and 27 rnds = 4" in Moss St in the rnd, blocked
52 sts = 8.5" over Body Cable Panel in the rnd, blocked

For pattern support, contact kristen@kristentendyke.com

Julie's Sweater

Notes:
The body is worked in the round from the bottom up to the underarm, where the back and front are divided and worked separately, back and forth in rows, to the shoulders. The shoulders are joined with a three-needle bind-off then the stitches for the sleeves are picked up around the armholes. Sleeve caps are shaped with short-rows, then knit down to the cuff. Thumbholes are worked in the ribbing at each sleeve cuff.

Use different colored markers for beginning of round, cable panel and side of body to easily tell them apart. When working charts flat, read RS rows (odd numbers) from right to left, and WS rows (even numbers) from left to right. When working charts in the rnd, read all chart rows from right to left, as RS rows.

Keeping in Pattern While Decreasing
Decreasing before the M: if the next st on the left needle is a knit st, then SSK; if the next st on the left needle is a purl st, then SSP. Decreasing after the M: if the second st on the left needle is a knit st, then K2tog; if the second st on the left needle is a purl st, then P2tog. It doesn't matter if the first st on the left needle is knit or purl because this is the st that is being decreased.

Keeping in Pattern while Increasing
For the first inc: If pattern is established as: K1, P2, SM, K1, P2, work inc's as: K1, M1P, P2, SM, K1, M1, P2. If pattern is established as: P2, K2, SM, P2, K2, work inc's as: P2, M1, K2, SM, P2, M1P, K2.
For the second inc: If pattern is established as K2, p3, SM, k3, P2, work inc's as: K2, P1, M1P, P2, SM, K2, M1, K1, P2. If pattern is established as P2, k3, SM, p3, K2, work inc's as: P2, K1, M1, K2, SM, P2, M1P, P1, K2.
For the third inc: If pattern is established as K2, P4, SM, K4, P2, work inc's as: K2, P2, M1, P2, SM, K2, M1P, K2, P2. If pattern is established as P2, K4, SM, P4, K2, work inc's as: P2, K2, M1P, K2, SM, P2, M1, P2, K2.
For the fourth inc: If pattern is established as K2, P2, K1, P2, SM, K2, P1, K2, P2, work inc's as: K2, P2, K1, M1, P2, SM, K2, M1P, P1, K2, P2. If pattern is established as P2, K2, P1, K2, SM, P2, K1, P2, K2, work inc's as: P2, K2, P1, M1P, K2, SM, P2, M1, K1, P2, K2.

Moss St (in the rnd over a multiple of 4 sts plus 2):
Rnds 1 and 2: P2, *K2, P2; rep from * to end.
Rnds 3 and 4: K2, *P2, K2; rep from * to end.
Rep Rnds 1-4 for pattern.

Moss St (worked flat over a multiple of 4 sts plus 2):
Row 1: P2, *K2, P2; rep from * to end.
Row 2: K2, *P2, K2; rep from * to end.
Row 3: K2, *P2, K2; rep from * to end.
Row 4: P2, *K2, P2; rep from * to end.
Rep Rows 1-4 for pattern.

Body Cable Panel (in the rnd over 52 sts):
Rnd 1: P2, 4/4RC, P2, K2, P8, K4, P8, K2, P2, 4/4LC, P2.
Rnd 2: P2, K8, P2, K2, P8, K4, P8, K2, P2, K8, P2.
Rnd 3: P2, K8, P2, 2/2LPC, P8, 2/2RC, P8, 2/2RPC, P2, K8, P2.
Rnd 4: P2, K8, P4, K2, P8, K4, P8, K2, P4, K8, P2.
Rnd 5: P2, K8, P4, (2/2LPC, P4, 2/2RPC) twice, P4, K8, P2.
Rnd 6: P2, K8, P6, (K2, P4) 4 times, P2, K8, P2.
Rnd 7: P2, K8, P6, (2/2LPC, 2/2RPC, P4) twice, P2, K8, P2.
Rnd 8: P2, K8, P8, (K4, P8) twice, K8, P2.
Rnd 9: P2, 4/4RC, P8, 2/2LC, P8, 2/2RC, P8, 4/4LC, P2.
Rnd 10: Rep Rnd 8.
Rnd 11: P2, K8, P6, (2/2RPC, 2/2LPC, P4) twice, P2, K8, P2.
Rnd 12: Rep Rnd 6.
Rnd 13: P2, K8, P4, (2/2RPC, P4, 2/2LPC) twice, P4, K8, P2.
Rnd 14: Rep Rnd 4.
Rnd 15: P2, K8, P2, 2/2RPC, P8, 2/2RC, P8, 2/2LPC, P2, K8, P2.
Rnd 16: Rep Rnd 2.
Rep Rnds 1-16 for pattern.

Body Cable Panel: (worked flat over 52 sts)
Row 1 (RS): P2, 4/4RC, P2, K2, P8, K4, P8, K2, P2, 4/4LC, P2.
Row 2 (WS): K2, P8, K2, P2, K8, P4, K8, P2, K2, P8, K2.
Row 3: P2, K8, P2, 2/2LPC, P8, 2/2RC, P8, 2/2RPC, P2, K8, P2.
Row 4: K2, P8, K4, P2, K8, P4, K8, P2, K4, P8, K2.
Row 5: P2, K8, P4, (2/2LPC, P4, 2/2RPC) twice, P4, K8, P2.
Row 6: K2, P8, K6, (P2, K4) 4 times, K2, P8, K2.
Row 7: P2, K8, P6, (2/2LPC, 2/2RPC, P4) twice, P2, K8, P2.
Row 8: K2, P8, K8, (P4, K8) twice, P8, K2.
Row 9: P2, 4/4RC, P8, 2/2LC, P8, 2/2RC, P8, 4/4LC, P2.
Row 10: Rep Row 8.
Row 11: P2, K8, P6, (2/2RPC, 2/2LPC, P4) twice, P2, K8, P2.
Row 12: Rep Row 6.
Row 13: P2, K8, P4, (2/2RPC, P4, 2/2LPC) twice, P4, K8, P2.
Row 14: Rep Row 4.
Row 15: P2, K8, P2, 2/2RPC, P8, 2/2RC, P8, 2/2LPC, P2, K8, P2.
Row 16: Rep Row 2.
Rep Rows 1-16 for pattern.

Right Sleeve Cable Panel (worked flat over 12 sts)
Row 1 (RS): P2, 4/4RC, P2.
Rows 2, 4, 6 and 8 (WS): K2, P8, K2.
Rows 3, 5 and 7: P2, K8, P2.
Rep Rows 1-8 for pattern.

Right Sleeve Cable Panel (in the rnd over 12 sts)
Rnd 1: P2, 4/4RC, P2.
Rnds 2-8: P2, K8, P2.
Rep Rnds 1-8 for pattern.

Left Sleeve Cable Panel (worked flat over 12 sts) (also, see chart)
Row 1 (RS): P2, 4/4LC, P2.
Rows 2, 4, 6 and 8 (WS): K2, P8, K2.
Rows 3, 5 and 7: P2, K8, P2.
Rep Rows 1-8 for pattern.

Left Sleeve Cable Panel (in the rnd over 12 sts)
Rnd 1: P2, 4/4LC, P2.
Rnds 2-8: P2, K8, P2.
Rep Rnds 1-8 for pattern.

Three Needle Bind Off Method: With an equal number of sts on 2 separate needles; with the RS of garment pieces tog (to form ridge on inside of garment), hold the needles parallel. With a third needle K the first st of front and back needles together, *K next st from each needle together, (2 sts on RH needle), BO 1 st; rep from * until all sts are BO.

Short-Rows, Wrap and Turn (W&T):
Knit row: WYIB, Sl next st P-wise onto RH needle, bring yarn to front of work, return slipped st to LH needle, bring yarn to back of work, then turn work.
Purl row: WYIF Sl next st P-wise onto RH needle, bring yarn to back of work, return slipped st to LH needle, bring yarn to front of work, then turn work.

Hide Wraps:
Knit row: PU the wrap from the front with the RH needle and K tog with the st it wraps.
Purl row: PU the wrap TBL with RH needle and P tog with the st it wraps.

2/2LC: Sl 2 sts to CN, hold in front, K2; K2 from CN.
2/2RC: Sl 2 sts to CN, hold in back, K2; K2 from CN.
2/2LPC: Sl 2 sts to CN, hold in front, P2; K2 from CN.
2/2RPC: Sl 2 sts to CN, hold in back, K2; P2 from CN.
4/4LC: Sl 4 sts to CN, hold in front, K4; K4 from CN.
4/4RC: Sl 4 sts to CN, hold in back, K4; K4 from CN.

K2, P2 Ribbing (worked in the rnd over a multiple of 4 sts):
All Rnds: *K2, P2; rep from * around.

DIRECTIONS
Body
The body is worked in the rnd from the bottom up to the underarms.
With longer circular needle, CO 138 (154, 170, 186, 202, 218, 234, 250, 266) sts. PM for beginning of rnd and join to work in the rnd, being careful not to twist sts.

Establish Ribbing: (K2, P2) 3 (4, 5, 6, 7, 8, 9, 10, 11) times, K2, PM for cable panel, (P2, K2) twice, (P2, K4) 5 times, (P2, K2) twice, P2, PM for cable panel, (K2, P2) to end.
Cont working in ribbing as established until piece measures 3" from CO edge.

Inc Rnd: Work in ribbing as established to M, SM, P2, (K1, M1) twice, P2, K2, (P2, K4) 5 times, P2, K2, P2, (M1, K1) twice, P2, SM, work in ribbing as established to end. 142 (158, 174, 190, 206, 222, 238, 254, 270) sts.

Establish Pattern: Work in Moss St to M, SM, work Body Cable Chart to next M, SM, work in Moss St to end. Cont working in pattern as established until piece measures 5" from CO edge, ending after an even numbered rnd of patterns.

Shape Waist
Set-up Rnd: Work in Moss St to M, SM, work Body Cable Chart to next M, SM, work 14 (18, 22, 26, 30, 34, 38, 42, 46) sts in Moss St, PM for side, cont in Moss St to end. 80 (88, 96, 104, 112, 120, 128, 136, 144) sts for front and 62 (70, 78, 86, 94, 102, 110, 118, 126) sts for back.

Dec Rnd: *K2tog or P2tog keeping in pattern (see Notes), work as established to 2 sts before side M, SSK or SSP keeping in pattern, SM; rep from * once more. 4 sts dec.
Work 9 rnds even as established.
Rep the last 10 rnds 3 more times. 126 (142, 158, 174, 190, 206, 222, 238, 254) sts remain; 72 (80, 88, 96, 104, 112, 120, 128, 136) sts for front and 54 (62, 70, 78, 86, 94, 102, 110, 118) sts for back.

Work 8 rnds even.

Inc Rnd: *Work 2 sts in Moss St as established, M1 or M1P keeping in pattern (see Notes), work as established to 2 sts before side M, M1 or M1P keeping in pattern, work 2 sts in Moss St as established, SM; rep from * once more. 4 sts inc.
Work 7 rnds even as established, working inc sts into Moss st as they appear.
Rep the last 8 rnds 3 more times. 142 (158, 174, 190, 206, 222, 238, 254, 270) sts; 80 (88, 96, 104, 112, 120, 128, 136, 144) sts for front and 62 (70, 78, 86, 94, 102, 110, 118, 126) sts for back.

Cont working even as established until piece measures 19" from CO edge, ending after an even numbered rnd of patterns, ending the last rnd 3 (3, 4, 4, 5, 5, 6, 7, 8) sts before end of rnd.

Divide Back and Front: BO next 6 (6, 8, 8, 10, 10, 12, 14, 16) sts removing the beginning of rnd M, work as established to 3 (3, 4, 4, 5, 5, 6, 7, 8) sts before side M, BO 6 (6, 8, 8, 10, 10, 12, 14, 16) sts removing side M, work to end as established. 74 (82, 88, 96, 102, 110, 116, 122, 128) sts remain for front and 56 (64, 70, 78, 84, 92, 98, 104, 110) sts remain for back. Place front sts onto st holder or scrap yarn and cont working back and forth on back sts only.

Back
Shape Armholes
Next Row (WS): Sl 1 st P-wise WYIF, work in Moss St as established to last st, P1.
Dec Row (RS): Sl 1 st P-wise WYIB, K2tog or P2tog keeping in pattern, work in Moss St as established to last 3 sts, SSK or SSP keeping in pattern, K1. 2 sts dec.
Rep the last 2 rows 3 (6, 7, 10, 11, 14, 15, 17, 18) more times. 48 (50, 54, 56, 60, 62, 66, 68, 72) sts.

Cont working even in Moss St, slipping the first st of every row, until armholes measure 6 (6.75, 6.75, 7.5, 7.5, 8, 8, 8.75, 8.75)" from divide, ending after a WS row.

Shape Neck
Next Row (RS): Sl 1 st P-wise WYIB, work 9 (10, 12, 12, 14, 15, 16, 17, 19) sts in Moss St as established, join a second ball of yarn and BO 28 (28, 28, 30, 30, 30, 32, 32, 32) sts, then work in Moss st to last st as established, K1. 10 (11, 13, 13, 15, 16, 17, 18, 20) sts remain on each side.

Work both sides at the same time with separate balls of yarn as follows:
Next Row (WS): Sl 1 st P-wise WYIF, work in Moss St to 1 st before neck edge, P1; on other side, Sl 1 st P-wise WYIF, work in Moss St to last st, P1.

Dec Row (RS): Sl 1 st P-wise WYIB, work in Moss St to 3 sts before neck edge, SSK or SSP keeping in pattern, K1; on other side, Sl 1 st P-wise WYIB, K2tog or P2tog keeping in pattern, work in Moss st to last st, K1. 1 st dec on each side. Rep the last 2 rows 2 more times. 7 (8, 10, 10, 12, 13, 14, 15, 17) sts. Work 1 more WS row even as established.

Shape Shoulders with Short-Rows
Short-Row 1 (RS): *Work as established to neck edge; on other side, work to last 2 (3, 3, 3, 4, 4, 5, 5, 6) sts, W&T.
Short-Row 2 (WS): *Work as established to neck edge; on other side, work to last 2 (3, 3, 3, 4, 4, 5, 5, 6) sts, W&T.
Short-Row 3 (RS): *Work as established to neck edge; on other side, work to last 5 (5, 7, 7, 8, 9, 9, 10, 11) sts, W&T.
Short-Row 4 (WS): *Work as established to neck edge; on other side, work to last 5 (5, 7, 7, 8, 9, 9, 10, 11) sts, W&T.
Next Row (RS): Work as established to neck edge; on other side, K to end working wraps tog with their sts as they appear.
Next Row (WS): Purl to neck edge; on other side, purl to end working wraps tog with their sts as they appear.
Break yarn and place sts onto st holders or scrap yarn.

Front
Return 74 (82, 88, 96, 102, 110, 116, 122, 128) held front sts to needle and join yarn preparing to work a WS row.

Shape Armholes
Next Row (WS): Sl 1 st P-wise WYIF, work as established to last st, P1.
Dec Row (RS): Sl 1 st P-wise WYIB, K2tog or P2tog keeping in pattern, work as established to last 3 sts, SSK or SSP keeping in pattern, K1. 2 sts dec.
Rep the last 2 rows 3 (6, 7, 10, 11, 14, 15, 17, 18) more times. 66 (68, 72, 74, 78, 80, 84, 86, 90) sts.

Cont working even as established, slipping the first st of every row, until armholes measure 4 (4.75, 4.75, 5.5, 5.5, 6, 6, 6.75, 6.75)" from divide, ending after a WS row.

Shape Neck
Next Row (RS): Sl 1 st P-wise WYIB, work 14 (15, 17, 17, 19, 20, 21, 22, 24) sts as established, join a second ball of yarn and BO 36 (36, 36, 38, 38, 38, 40, 40, 40) sts, then work as established to last st, K1. 15 (16, 18, 18, 20, 21, 22, 23, 25) sts remain on each side.

Work both sides at the same time with separate balls of yarn as follows:
Next Row: Work as established to neck edge; on other side, BO 4 sts, work to end.
Work last row once more. 11 (12, 14, 14, 16, 17, 18, 19, 21) sts rem on each side.

Next Row (WS): Sl 1 st P-wise WYIF, work as established to 1 st before neck edge, P1; on other side, Sl 1 st P-wise WYIF, work as established to last st, P1.

Dec Row (RS): Sl 1 st P-wise WYIB, work as established to 3 sts before neck edge, SSK or SSP keeping in pattern, K1; on other side, Sl 1 st P-wise WYIB, K2tog or P2tog keeping in pattern, work as established st to last st, K1. 1 st dec'd on each side.

Rep the last 2 rows 3 more times. 7 (8, 10, 10, 12, 13, 14, 15, 17) sts. Work 1 more WS row even as established.

Cont working even as established, slipping the first st of every row, until armholes measure 7 (7.75, 7.75, 8.5, 8.5, 9, 9, 9.75, 9.75)" from divide, ending after a WS row.

Shape Shoulders with Short-Rows
Same as for back.

Join Shoulders
Return 7 (8, 10, 10, 12, 13, 14, 15, 17) held back sts from each shoulder to DPNs, then use the Three Needle Bind Off Method to join the back and front shoulders together. Rep for second shoulder.

Right Sleeve
With 16" circular or DPNs and RS facing, beginning at center of right underarm, PU 3 (3, 4, 4, 5, 5, 6, 7, 8) sts along underarm BO sts, then 21 (25, 24, 28, 27, 31, 30, 33, 32) sts evenly along armhole edge to shoulder, then PU 21 (25, 24, 28, 27, 31, 30, 33, 32) sts evenly along armhole edge to BO sts, PU 3 (3, 4, 4, 5, 5, 6, 7, 8) sts along remaining BO sts. 48 (56, 56, 64, 64, 72, 72, 80, 80) sts. PM for beginning of rnd and join for working in the rnd.

Establish Pattern and Shape Cap with Short-rows
Short-Row 1 (RS): Work 18 (22, 22, 26, 26, 30, 30, 34, 34) sts in Moss St, PM for cable panel, work 12 sts in Right Sleeve Chart, PM for cable panel, W&T.
Short-Row 2 (WS): SM, work in Right Sleeve Chart to next M, SM, W&T. 17 (21, 21, 25, 25, 29, 29, 33, 33) sts remain unworked at each end of rnd.
Short-Row 3 (RS): SM, work in Right Sleeve Chart to next M, SM, work next st in Moss St, working it tog with its wrap, work 1 more st in Moss St, W&T.
Short-Row 4 (WS): Work to M in Moss St, SM, work to next M in Right Sleeve Chart, SM, work next st in Moss St, working it tog with its wrap, work 1 more st in Moss St, W&T. 15 (19, 19, 23, 23, 27, 27, 31, 31) sts remain unworked at each end of rnd.
Short-Row 5 (RS): Maintaining Right Sleeve Chart between markers and working Moss St outside the markers, work as established to wrapped st from previous row, work it tog with its wrap, work 1 more st, W&T.
Short-Row 6 (WS): Work as established to wrapped st, work it tog with its wrap, work 1 more st, W&T.
Rep the Short-Rows 5 and 6 1 (4, 3, 6, 5, 8, 7, 10, 9) more times. 11 (9, 11, 9, 11, 9, 11, 9, 11) sts remain unworked at each end of rnd.
Short-Row 7 (RS): Work as established to wrapped st from previous row, work it tog with its wrap, W&T.
Short-Row 8 (WS): Work as established to wrapped st, work it tog with its wrap, W&T.

Rep the last Short-Rows 7 and 8 7 (5, 6, 4, 5, 3, 4, 1, 2) more times. 3 (3, 4, 4, 5, 5, 6, 7, 8) sts remain unworked at each end of the rnd.

Next Row (RS): Work as established to end, working the wrap tog with its st as you come to it. Do not turn work, begin working in the rnd.

Next Rnd: Work in Moss St to M, SM, work in Right Sleeve Chart to next M, SM, work in Moss St to end of rnd working the wrap tog with its st as you come to it.

Cont working in the rnd until piece measures 1" from underarm, ending after an odd numbered rnd of patterns.

Shape Sleeve

(Note: If using shorter circular needle, change to DPNs when sts no longer fit comfortably on circular needle.)

Dec Rnd: K2tog or P2tog keeping in pattern, work as established to last 2 sts, SSK or SSP keeping in pattern. 2 sts dec.

Work 13 (8, 8, 7, 7, 5, 5, 4, 4) rnds even in pattern.

Rep the last 14 (9, 9, 8, 8, 6, 6, 5, 5) rnds 7 (11, 11, 13, 13, 17, 17, 19, 19) more times. 32 (32, 32, 36, 36, 36, 36, 40, 40) sts.

Cont working even as established until piece measures 18" from underarm, ending after an even numbered rnd of patterns.

Work in K2, P2 Rib for 2".

Shape Thumb Hole

Set-up Row (RS): Work in ribbing as established to last 5 sts, PM for thumbhole, turn, leaving remaining sts unworked. Cont working back and forth in rows as follows:

Row 1 (WS): Sl 1 st P-wise WYIF, work in ribbing to end of rnd, then cont to thumbhole M, turn.

Row 2 (RS): Sl 1 st P-wise WYIB, work in ribbing to beginning of rnd, then cont to thumbhole M, turn.

Rep the last 2 rows 3 more times, do not turn after last RS row.

Next Rnd: With RS still facing, remove thumbhole M and rejoin to work in the rnd, cont in ribbing as established to end of rnd.

Cont working in ribbing as established until ribbing measures 5" total and sleeve measures 23" from underarm.

BO all sts loosely in ribbing.

Left Sleeve

Work same as for right sleeve, working Left Sleeve Chart in place of Right Sleeve Chart, until piece measures 18" from underarm, ending after an even numbered rnd of patterns.

Work in K2, P2 Rib for 2".

Shape Thumb Hole

Set-up Row (RS): Work 5 sts in ribbing, PM for thumbhole, turn, leaving remaining sts unworked. Cont as for right sleeve thumbhole.

Finishing

Block piece to measurements.

Collar

With shorter circular needle and RS facing, beginning at right shoulder, PU 6 sts evenly along right back neck edge, 28 (28, 28, 30, 30, 30, 32, 32, 32) sts along back neck BO sts, 6 sts evenly along left back neck edge to shoulder, 14 sts along left front edge, 44 (44, 44, 46, 46, 46, 48, 48, 48) sts along center front BO sts, then 14 sts along right front edge to shoulder. 112 (112, 112, 116, 116, 116, 120, 120, 120) sts. PM for beginning of rnd, then join to work in the rnd.

Dec Rnd: *K2, P2, K2tog, K1, P2; rep from * 11 more times, (K2, P2) 1 (1, 1, 2, 2, 2, 3, 3, 3) more times. 100 (100, 100, 104, 104, 104, 108, 108, 108) sts.

Work in K2, P2 ribbing until piece measures 10" from pick-up rnd, or for desired length. BO all sts loosely in ribbing.

Weave in ends.
Block again if desired.

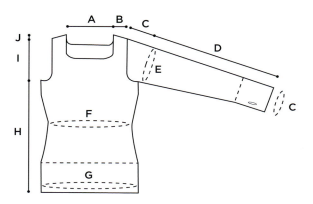

A 8.5 (8.5, 8.5, 9, 9, 9, 9.5, 9.5, 9.5)"
B 1.75 (4, 4, 4.25, 4.25, 4.5, 4.5, 4.5, 4.5)"
C 3.75 (4, 4, 4.25, 4.25, 4.5, 4.5, 4.5, 4.5)"
D 23"
E 12 (14, 14, 16, 16, 18, 18, 20, 20)"
F 27 (31, 35, 39, 43, 47, 51, 55, 59)"
G 31 (35, 39, 43, 47, 51, 55, 59, 63)"
H 19"
I 7 (7.75, 7.75, 8.5, 8.5, 9, 9, 9.75, 9.75)"
J 1"

Body Cable Chart

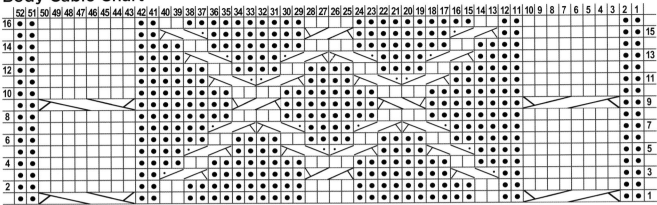

Left Sleeve Cable

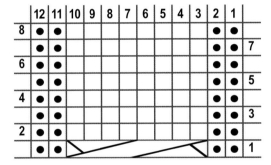

Right Sleeve Chart

Legend:

knit
RS: knit stitch
WS: purl stitch

purl
RS: purl stitch
WS: knit stitch

c2 over 2 left
SL2 to CN, hold in front.
K2, K2 from CN

c2 over 2 right
SL2 to CN, hold in back.
K2, K2 from CN

c2 over 2 left purl
SL2 to CN, hold in front.
P2, K2 from CN

c2 over 2 right purl
SL2 to CN, hold in back.
K2, P2 from CN

c4 over 4 left
SL4 to CN, hold in front.
K4, K4 from CN

c4 over 4 right
SL4 to CN, hold in back.
K4, then K4 from CN

Julie's Sweater

STRAIGHT & ARROW CARDIGAN

by Stacey Gerbman

FINISHED MEASUREMENTS
36.75 (39.5, 41.5, 43.5, 47.5, 49.5)" finished bust measurement; garment is meant to be worn with 2-4" of positive ease

YARN
Knit Picks Wool of the Andes Superwash Worsted (100% Superwash Wool; 110 yards/50g): Fjord Heather 26316, 13 (14, 15, 16, 17, 18) balls

NEEDLES
US 8 (5mm) 16, 32, and 40" circular needles, or size to obtain gauge

NOTIONS
Yarn Needle, Stitch Markers, Cable Needle, Scrap Yarn or Stitch Holder

GAUGE
18 sts and 29 rows = 4" in Garter Rib pattern, blocked
19 sts and 30 rows = 4" in Straight and Arrow cable pattern, blocked
21 sts and 24 rows = 4" in K2, P2 Rib, blocked

For pattern support, contact staceygerbman@gmail.com

Straight & Arrow Cardigan

Notes:
The body of this open front cardigan is knit flat to the armholes, then the two front sections and the back are worked separately to the shoulder. The sleeves are worked flat, and then seamed and sewn into the body armholes. The front bands and collar are picked up and knit back and forth shaping the shawl collar with the Yarn Over Method of short rows.

The Straight and Arrow Chart is worked back and forth in panels on both the front and back of the cardigan. When reading the chart, read RS rows from right to left, and WS rows from left to right. The total pattern repeat happens over 12 rows. There are two 4-stitch cables, two antler cables, and a textured mock cable pattern in the center. Instructions have you place markers at the beginning and end of the full chart; however, you may want to add different colored markers between each section of the chart to identify each part of the larger chart. As you bind off stitches for the shoulder and neck, as soon as you begin to decrease into a cable work the rest of the chart section as if it were Stockinette.

2/2 LC: Sl 2 sts to CN, hold to front, K2, K2 from CN.
1/2 LC: Sl 1 st to CN, hold in front, K2, K1 from CN.
1/2 RC: Sl 2 sts to CN, hold in back, K1, K2 from CN.

Garter Stitch (worked flat over any number of sts)
All Rows: Knit.

K2, P2 Rib (worked flat over multiples of 4 sts plus 2 sts for Body and Collar, multiples of 4 sts for Sleeves)
Row 1 (RS): (K2, P2) to end for Sleeves, or to last 2 sts, K2, for Body and Collar.
Row 2 (WS): (P2, K2), to end for Sleeves, or to last 2 sts, P2, for Body and Collar.
Rep Rows 1-2 for pattern.

K1, P1 Rib (worked flat over multiple of 2 sts)
Row 1 (RS): *K1, P1, rep from * to the end of row.
Row 2 (WS): *P1, K1, rep from * to the end of row.
Rep Rows 1-2 for pattern.

Garter Rib (worked flat over multiples of 6 sts plus 3 for Body, multiples of 6 sts for Sleeves)
Row 1 (RS): Knit.
Row 2 (WS): (K3, P3) to end for Sleeves, or to last 3 sts, K3, for Body.
Rep Rows 1-2 for pattern.

Chart 1, Straight and Arrow Chart (worked flat over 36 sts)
Row 1 (RS): K6, P1, K1, P1, K4, P3, K2, P2, K7, P1, K1, P1, K6.
Row 2 (WS): P6, K1, P1, K1, P6, K2, P1, K1, P2, K2, P4, K1, P1, K1, P6.
Row 3: K6, P1, K1, P1, 2/2 LC, P1, K2, P2, K2, P2, K1, 2/2 LC, P1, K1, P1, K6.
Row 4: P6, K1, P1, K1, P4, K2, P3, K3, P6, K1, P1, K1, P6.
Row 5: 1/2 LC, 1/2 RC, P1, K1, P1, K5, P4, K4, P1, K4, P1, K1, P1, 1/2 LC, 1/2 RC.
Row 6: P6, K1, P1, K1, P8, K1, P1, K4, P4, K1, P1, K1, P6.
Row 7: K6, P1, K1, P1, 2/2 LC, P3, K2, P2, K3, 2/2 LC, P1, K1, P1, K6.
Row 8: Rep Row 2.
Row 9: K6, P1, K1, P1, K4, P1, (K2, P2) twice, K5, P1, K1, P1, K6.
Row 10: Rep Row 4.
Row 11: 1/2 LC, 1/2 RC, P1, K1, P1, 2/2 LC, K1, P4, K4, P1, 2/2 LC, P1, K1, P1, 1/2 LC, 1/2 RC.
Row 12: Rep Row 6.
Rep Rows 1-12 for pattern.

Sloped Bind Off
Step 1: Work the first BO rows at the garment edges as usual.
Step 2: One row before the next BO row, work to the last st of the row, turn.
Step 3: Slip the first st from the LH needle P-wise, pass the unworked st of the previous row over the slipped st (the first st is bound off). BO remaining sts as usual.
Rep Steps 2-3 for remaining BO rows.

Short Rows Yarn Over Method
Turn & YO on either a RS or WS Row: Work to specified point, turn work (opposite side facing now), then, if next st on LH needle is a P, bring yarn back between LH and RH needles, bring yarn forward over RH needle (making a YO). Now prepare to P the next st. YO will rest next to the turning point. If the next st on the LH needle is a K st, bring yarn to front between LH and RH needles, bring yarn to back over RH needle (making a YO), now prepare to K the next st. YO will rest next to the turning point.

The YO must not be twisted or crossed on the needle, as that will make it more difficult to hide on subsequent rows.

To Hide YO in Subsequent Rows on either a RS or WS Row: Work to the YO, then, if the st following YO is a K st, insert R needle into first unworked st on LH needle (after YO) and into YO, knit these two together. If the st following YO is a P st, SSP the YO together with the next st on the LH needle.

Backward Loop CO: *Use the working yarn to make a loop around your left thumb, then place this loop onto the RH needle; repeat from * until you have the required number of sts on your needle.

DIRECTIONS
Pocket Linings (make 2 the same)
CO 24 sts with 16" circular needle. Work flat in St st (K on RS, P on WS) for 4". Place sts on holder.

Body
CO 174 (186, 202, 218, 238, 250) sts with 32" or 40" circular needle.
Work K2, P2 Rib for 2", ending with a RS row,
Decrease Row (WS): P all sts decreasing 18 (18, 26, 32, 34, 36) sts evenly across row. 156 (168, 176, 186, 204, 214) sts.

Torso
Set-up Row (RS): K3 (3, 1, 6, 3, 2), PM(1), work Row 1 of Straight and Arrow Chart across next 36 sts, PM(2), work Row 1 of Garter Rib pattern over next 21 (27, 33, 33, 45, 51) sts, PM(3), work Row 1 of Straight and Arrow Chart across next 36 sts, PM(4), work Row 1 of Garter Rib pattern over next 21 (27, 33, 33, 45, 51) sts, PM(5), work Row 1 of Straight

and Arrow Chart over next 36 sts, PM(6), K3 (3, 1, 6, 3, 2).

Work across sts, following chart as set. Maintain the sts before first and after last marker in Garter St. Work 2-row rep for Garter Rib, and 12-row rep for Straight and Arrow Chart ending with a WS row when piece measures 6" from CO edge.

Pocket Placement

K3 (3, 1, 6, 3, 2), SM(1), work first 6 sts of Straight and Arrow Chart, place next 24 sts on a holder, with RS of pocket lining facing you work 24 sts of Straight and Arrow Chart over one of the pocket linings, finish with remaining 6 sts of Straight and Arrow Chart. SM(2), work Row 1 of Garter Rib pattern over next 21 (27, 33, 33, 45, 51) sts, SM(3), work Row 1 of Straight and Arrow Chart across next 36 sts, SM(4), work Row 1 of Garter Rib pattern over next 21 (27, 33, 33, 45, 51) sts, SM(5), work first 6 sts of Straight and Arrow Chart, place next 24 sts on holder, with RS of pocket lining facing you work 24 sts of Straight and Arrow Chart over pocket lining, finish with remaining 6 sts of Straight and Arrow Chart, SM(6), K3 (3, 1, 6, 3, 2).

Work sweater in pattern until piece measures 16.5 (17, 17.25, 17.25, 17.25, 17.25)" from CO edge or desired length to underarm, ending with a WS row.

Divide for Fronts and Back

Work in pattern across first 39 (42, 43, 45, 48, 50) sts for right front, transfer next 78 (84, 90, 96, 108, 114) sts to stitch holder or scrap yarn for back, then transfer last 39 (42, 43, 45, 48, 50) sts to separate stitch holder or scrap yarn for left front.

Right Front
Shape Armhole and Front Neck

Armhole and neck shaping are worked at the same time. Armhole shaping will begin first, and will continue during neck shaping. Please read the following section through to the end, and review Sloped Bind Off before proceeding.

BO 4 (4, 4, 4, 4, 5) sts at the beginning of the next WS row, then BO 3 (4, 4, 4, 4, 4) sts at the beginning of the following WS row, then BO 2 (2, 3, 3, 3, 4) sts at the beginning of the following WS row, then BO 2 (1, 3, 3, 3, 4) sts at the beginning of the following WS row, then BO 0 (0, 0, 1, 1, 1) st at the beginning of the following 0 (0, 0, 1, 3, 5) WS rows.

AT THE SAME TIME, when armhole measures 1.5 (1.75, 1.75, 2.25, 2, 2.25)" ending with a WS row, shape neck as follows:

Neck Decrease Row (RS): K1, SSK, work as established to end, continue armhole shaping if necessary. 1 st dec at neck edge. Repeat the Neck Decrease Row every RS row 10 (10, 5, 4, 0, 0) more times, then every 4th row 5 (5, 9, 9, 11, 5) times, then every 6th row 0 (0, 0, 0, 0, 4) times, keeping 1 st at neck edge in Garter St.

Upon completion of all shaping, you will have bound off a total of 11 (11, 14, 15, 17, 22) sts at armhole edge and will have worked the Neck Decrease Row a total of 16 (16, 15, 14, 12, 10) times. 12 (15, 14, 16, 19, 18) sts.

Work even as established over remaining sts until armhole measures 7.5 (7.75, 8.5, 9, 9.25, 9.5)" ending with a RS row.

Shape Shoulder

Use the sloped Bind Off in this section for best results. BO 4 (4, 4, 4, 5, 5) sts at the beginning of the next 2 WS rows, then BO 2 (4, 3, 4, 5, 4) sts at the beginning of the following WS row, then BO 2 (3, 3, 4, 4, 4) sts at the beginning of following WS row.

Back

Transfer held 78 (84, 90, 96, 108, 114) back sts to needle and rejoin yarn ready to work a RS row.

Shape Armholes

Use the Sloped Bind Off in this section for best results. BO 4 (4, 4, 4, 4, 5) sts at the beginning of the next 2 rows, then BO 3 (4, 4, 4, 4, 4) sts at the beginning of the following 2 rows, then BO 2 (2, 3, 3, 3, 4) sts at the beginning of the following 2 rows, then BO 2 (1, 3, 3, 3, 4) st at the beginning of the following 2 rows, then BO 0 (0, 0, 1, 1, 1) st at the beginning of the following 0 (0, 0, 1, 3, 5) rows. 56 (62, 62, 66, 74, 70) sts.

Work even as established over remaining sts until armhole measures 7.5 (7.75, 8.5, 9, 9.25, 9.5)" ending with a WS row.

Shape Shoulders

Use the Sloped Bind Off in this section for best results. BO 4 (4, 4, 4, 5, 4) sts at the beginning of the next 4 rows, then BO 2 (4, 3, 4, 5, 4) sts at the beginning of the following 2 rows, then BO 2 (3, 3, 4, 4, 4) sts at the beginning of the following 2 rows.

Transfer remaining 32 (32, 34, 34, 36, 38) sts to stitch holder or scrap yarn for back neck.

Left Front

Transfer held 39 (42, 43, 45, 48, 50) left front sts to needle and rejoin yarn ready to work a RS row.

Shape Armhole and Front Neck

Armhole and neck shaping are worked at the same time. Armhole shaping will begin first, and will continue during neck shaping. Please read the following section through to the end. Please review Sloped Bind Off before proceeding.

BO 4 (4, 4, 4, 4, 5) sts at the beginning of the next RS row, then BO 3 (4, 4, 4, 4, 4) sts at the beginning of the following RS row, then BO 2 (2, 3, 3, 3, 4) sts at the beginning of the following RS row, then BO 2 (1, 3, 3, 3, 4) sts at the beginning of the following RS row, then BO 0 (0, 0, 1, 1, 1) st at the beginning of the following 0 (0, 0, 1, 3, 5) RS rows.

AT THE SAME TIME, when armhole measures 1.5 (1.75, 1.75, 2.25, 2, 2.25)" ending with a WS row, shape neck as follows:

Neck Decrease Row (RS): Work as established to last 3 sts, continuing armhole shaping if necessary, K2 tog, K1. 1 st dec at neck edge.

Repeat the Neck Decrease Row every RS row 10 (10, 5, 4, 0, 0) more times, then every 4th row 5 (5, 9, 9, 11, 5) times, then every 6th row 0 (0, 0, 0, 0, 4) times, keeping 1 st at neck edge in Garter St.

Upon completion of all shaping, you will have bound off a total of 11 (11, 14, 15, 17, 22) sts at armhole edge and will have worked the Neck Decrease Row a total of 16 (16, 15, 14, 12, 10) times. 12 (15, 14, 16, 19, 18) sts.

Work even as established over remaining sts until armhole measures 7.5 (7.75, 8.5, 9, 9.25, 9.5)" ending with a RS row.

Shape Shoulder
Use the sloped Bind Off in this section for best results.
BO 4 (4, 4, 4, 5, 5) sts at the beginning of the next 2 RS rows, then BO 2 (4, 3, 4, 5, 4) sts at the beginning of the following RS row, then BO 2 (3, 3, 4, 4, 4) sts at the beginning of following RS row.

Sleeves (make 2)
Loosely CO 46 (46, 50, 50, 54, 58) sts with 32" circular needle.
Work K2, P2 Rib for 2", ending with a RS row.
Decrease Row (WS): P all sts decreasing 4 (4, 2, 2, 6, 4) sts evenly across row. 42 (42, 48, 48, 48, 54) sts.
Work in Garter Rib pattern for 8 rows.

Shape Sleeve
Sleeve Increase Row (RS): K1, M1R, work as established to last st, M1L, K1. 2 sts inc.
Work a Sleeve Increase Row every 9 (8, 8, 7, 6, 8)th row 8 (6, 6, 2, 7, 10) times total, then every 0 (7, 10, 8, 9, 0)th row 0 (4, 3, 8, 4, 0) times.
Upon completion of this section you will have worked the Sleeve Increase Row a total of 8 (10, 9, 10, 11, 10) times. 58 (62, 66, 68, 70, 74) sts.
Work even in established pattern until piece measures 18 (18, 18.5, 18.5, 18.5, 18.75)" from CO edge, ending with a WS row.

Shape Cap
Use the Sloped Bind Off in this section for best results
BO 4 (4, 4, 3, 3, 3) sts at the beginning of the next 2 rows, then BO 3 (4, 3, 3, 3, 2) sts at the beginning of the following 2 rows, then BO 0 (2, 3, 2, 2, 2) sts at the beginning of the following 2 rows. 44 (42, 46, 52, 54, 60) sts.

Cap Decrease Row (RS): K1, K2tog, work as established to last 3 sts, SSK, K1. 2 sts dec.
Repeat the Cap Decrease Row every RS row 16 (15, 17, 19, 20, 21) times. 12 (12, 12, 14, 14, 18) sts.
BO all sts in pattern.

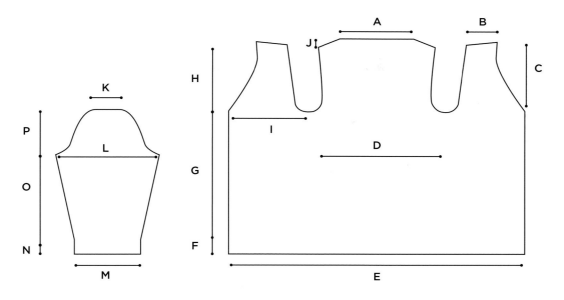

K 2.75(2.75, 2.75, 3, 3, 4)"
L 13 (13.75, 14.5, 15, 15.5, 16.5)"
M 8.75 (8.75, 9.5, 9.5, 10.25, 11)"
N 2"
O 16 (16, 16.5, 16.5, 16.5, 16.75)"
P 5.25 (5, 5.5, 6, 6.25, 6.5)"

A 6.75 (6.75, 7.25. 7.25, 7.5, 8)"
B 2.75 (3.25, 3, 3.5, 4.25, 4)"
C 7 .25 (7.25, 8, 8, 8.5, 8.5)"
D 17 (18.25, 19.5, 21 , 23.5, 25)"
E 33.5 (36, 37.75, 40, 44, 46.25)"
F 2"
G 14.5 (15, 15.25, 15.25, 15.25, 15.25)"
H 7.5 (7.75, 8.5, 9, 9.25, 9.5)"
I 8.25 (8.75, 9.5, 10, 10.5, 11.25)"
J 1"

Finishing

Sew the sides of the pocket linings to inside of the sweater (not the bottoms yet). PU 24 pocket sts and work K1, P1 Rib for 1.5". BO loosely and sew down edges to sweater front. Repeat with second pocket.

Weave in ends, wash and block to diagram. Sew shoulder seams. Sew bottoms of pocket linings to inside of sweater.

Collar

With 40" circular needle, RS facing and beginning at bottom of right front edge, PU and K 88 (92, 94, 96, 96, 96) sts evenly up right front to first neck decrease, PM(1), PU and K 39 (39, 42, 42, 45, 46) sts up right front neck edge to shoulder; transfer 32 (32, 34, 34, 36, 38) held back needle sts to LH needle tip and K across; PU and K 39 (39, 42, 42, 45, 46) sts down left front neck edge ending at first neck decrease, PM (2), PU and K 88 (92, 94, 96, 96, 96) sts down left front edge ending at CO edge. 286 (294, 306, 310, 318, 322) sts.

Next Row (WS): Work in K2, P2 Rib, starting with a WS Row 2.

Shape Collar

Please review Yarn Over Short Row Method before proceeding. Continue working in K2, P2 Rib.

Short Row 1 (RS): *Work in established rib to marker, SM; rep from * once, turn & YO;
Short Row 2 (WS): SM, work in established rib to marker, SM, turn & YO;
Short Row 3: Work in rib to 6 sts before YO from previous RS row, turn & YO;
Short Row 4: Work in rib to 6 sts before YO from previous WS row; turn & YO;
Short Rows 5-12: Rep Short Rows 3 & 4 four more times.
Row 13: Work in rib to end, working all short row YOs together with adjacent sts as described in Yarn Over Short Row Method.
Row 14: Work in rib to end, working all short row YOs together with adjacent sts.
Work 2 rows even in rib, ending with a WS row.
Rep Short Rows 1-14.
Work 3 rows even in rib, or until collar measures approximately 5.5" from pick up row, measured at back of neck.
Bind off all sts in pattern.

Sew sleeve seams. Set in sleeves.
Weave in any remaining ends invisibly on the WS of fabric. Gently steam collar or wet-block entire garment again.

Straight and Arrow Chart

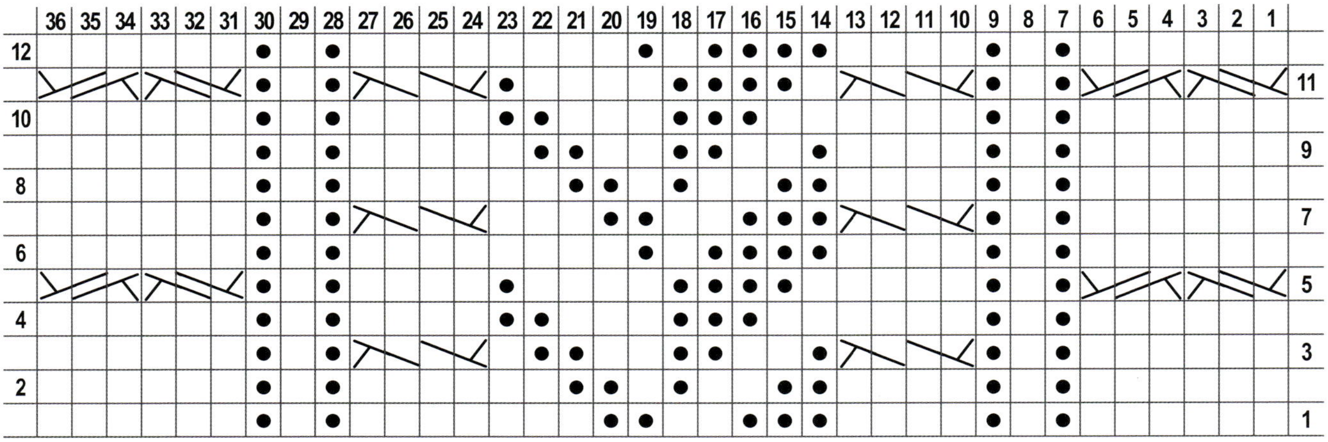

Legend:

- **knit**
  RS: knit stitch
  WS: purl stitch
- **purl**
  RS: purl stitch
  WS: knit stitch
- **c2 over 2 left**
  sl 2 to CN, hold in front. k2, k2 from CN
- **c1 over 2 left**
  sl 1 to CN, hold in front. k2, k1 from CN
- **c1 over 2 right**
  sl2 to CN, hold in back. k1, k2 from CN

COPAN HAT

by Joyce Fassbender

FINISHED MEASUREMENTS
22 inches circumference x 8.5 inches depth (blocked)

YARN
Knit Picks Hawthorne Tonal (80% Superwash Fine Highland Wool, 20% Polyamide (Nylon); 357 yards/100g) in Astoria 27411, 1 skein.

NEEDLES
US 1 (2.25mm) DPNs or 16" circular needles, or size to obtain gauge

US 3 (3.25mm) DPNs and 16" circular needles, or size to obtain gauge

NOTIONS
Yarn Needle, Stitch Markers, Cable needles

GAUGE
36 sts and 40 rows = 4" in Cable Pattern, blocked

For pattern support, contact joycef2@gmail.com

Copan Hat

Notes:
This hat is worked in the round from the bottom up, with a ribbed brim and intricate cable panels for the body. Ribbing is worked with smaller needles, while cabled body uses the larger size. Pattern is fully charted. Use stitch markers at beginning of round and between pattern repeats, if necessary.
In order to increase the depth of the hat, work additional repeats of rnds 1 – 22 of chart 2. Each additional repeat will add 2.5 inches to the length of the body.

DIRECTIONS

With smaller needles, cast on 198 stitches using a long-tail cast on. Place marker and join in the rnd taking care not to twist.

Ribbing
Work rnds 1 – 4 of chart 1 two times. Work chart nine (9) times per rnd. All charted rnds are worked from right to left.

Body
Switch to larger needles. Work rnds 1 – 22 of chart 2 two times. Work chart nine (9) times per rnd.

Crown
Work rnds 1 – 33 of chart 3 once. Work chart nine (9) times per rnd. Switch to DPNs as needed.
After completing chart 3, work one rnd as: (k2tog) four times, k1. 5 sts
Break yarn and run through remaining stitches.

Finishing
Weave in ends, wash and block.

Chart 1

Chart 2

Chart 3

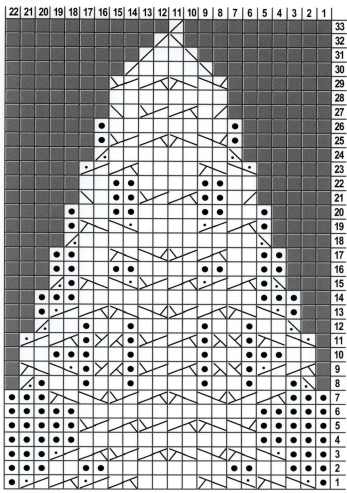

Legend:

- ● **purl** — purl stitch
- □ **knit** — knit stitch
- ▨ **no stitch**
- ◺ **K2TOG** — Knit two stitches together as one stitch
- ◸ **SSK** — Slip one stitch as if to knit, Slip another stitch as if to knit. Insert left-hand needle into front of these 2 stitches and knit them together
- ◺ **P2TOG** — Purl 2 stitches together
- ◸ **P2TOG TBL** — Purl two stitches together in back loops, inserting needle from the left, behind and into the backs of the 2nd & 1st stitches in that order
- **Right Twist** — Skip the first stitch, knit into 2nd stitch, then knit skipped stitch. Slip both stitches from needle together OR K2TOG leaving STS on LH needle, then K first ST again, SL both STS off needle
- **Left Twist** — SL1 to CN, hold in front. K1, K1 from CN
- **c2 over 2 left P** — SL2 to CN, hold in front. P2, K2 from CN
- **c2 over 2 right P** — SL2 to CN, hold in back. K2, P2 from CN
- **c2 over 2 left** — SL2 to CN, hold in front. K2, K2 from CN
- **c2 over 2 right** — SL2 to CN, hold in back. K2, K2 from CN

Copan Hat

CARRICK SHAWL

by Emily Dormier

FINISHED MEASUREMENTS
17.5 (27, 36)" wide x 80 (84, 88)" long

YARN
Knit Picks Wool of the Andes Tweed (80% Peruvian Highland Wool, 20% Donegal Tweed, 110 yards/50g): Brass Heather 25451, 14 (22, 30) balls

NEEDLES
US 7 (4.5mm) straight or circular needles, or size to obtain gauge

NOTIONS
Yarn Needle, Cable Needle

GAUGE
21 sts and 32 rows = 4" over Body Chart, blocked

For pattern support, contact emilydormier@gmail.com

Carrick Shawl

Notes:

This cozy rectangular shawl is perfect to throw over your shoulders year round. It features an all over cable design that is simple to make and gorgeous to look at.

The chart begins with a WS row, and is followed from right to left on RS rows (even numbers) and left to right on WS rows (odd numbers). The pattern repeat is worked 1 (2, 3) times.

DIRECTIONS

Body

Loosely CO 92 (140, 188) sts. Work Rows 1-16 from Body Chart, repeating them a total of 40 (42, 44) times.
BO in pattern.

Finishing

Weave in ends, wash and block.

Legend:

- □ **knit**
  RS: knit stitch
  WS: purl stitch
- ⊡ **purl**
  RS: purl stitch
  WS: knit stitch
- ▭ **pattern repeat**
- **c2 over 2 right**
  SL2 to CN, hold in back. K2, K2 from CN
- **c2 over 2 left P**
  SL2 to CN, hold in front. P2, K2 from CN
- **c2 over 2 left**
  SL2 to CN, hold in front. K2, K2 from CN
- **c2 over 2 right P**
  SL2 to CN, hold in back. K2, P2 from CN

Body Chart

SESTINA PULLOVER

by Cheryl Toy

FINISHED MEASUREMENTS
35.75 (40.25, 44.5, 48.75, 53, 58)" finished bust measurement; garment is meant to be worn with 4-6" of positive ease

YARN
Knit Picks Palette (100% Peruvian Highland Wool; 231 yards/50g): Hare Heather 26042, 7 (7, 7, 8, 8, 9, 9) balls

NEEDLES
US 4 (3.5mm) 32" circular needles and DPNs, or size to obtain gauge

US 2 (3mm) 24" circular needles, or two sizes smaller than size to obtain gauge

NOTIONS
Yarn Needle, Stitch Markers; 7 removable, 36 small fixed, 1 distinctive, Cable Needle, Scrap Yarn or Stitch Holders

GAUGE
32 sts and 36 rows = 4" in Cable Pattern on larger needles in the rnd, blocked
26 sts and 36 rows = 4" in Reverse St st and St st on larger needles in the rnd, blocked

For pattern support, contact cheryl@littlechurchknits.com

Sestina Pullover

Notes:
The Sestina Pullover is a classically styled raglan sweater worked from the top down. Featuring the airy quality of Knit Picks Palette, Sestina is a pullover that is delicate and decidedly feminine and highlighted with graceful, open cables. A trendy, slightly oversized fit and lyrical fabric drape make Sestina a versatile layering piece or a great stand-alone wardrobe staple.

Charts are worked in the round, reach each row from right to left as a RS row.

Knit-Purl Cast On Method
Make a slipknot and place it on the left needle. *Using the Knitted method, CO 1 st. This creates a knit st. Bring the right needle under the yarn to the back and insert the needle into the last st as if to purl. Purl the st and place on left needle. This creates a purl st. Rep from * for the required number of sts. The slipknot does not count in the CO st count.

Lifted Increase (LI)
Lift the st from the row below the first st on the left needle, placing on the left needle. Knit or purl the st as indicated (LI P-wise, or LI K-wise) in the pattern.

K1, P1 Ribbing (in the rnd over an even number of sts)
All Rnds: *K1, P1, rep from * to end of rnd.

RM: Removable section (stitch) marker.
PRM: Place removable stitch marker.
SRM: Slip removable stitch marker.
CM: Cable marker.
PCM: Place cable marker.
SCM: Slip cable marker.

DIRECTIONS

Yoke

Using the Knit-Purl method and smaller needles, CO 182 (194, 218, 230, 242, 254) sts. Place distinctive marker and join in the rnd by knitting the first st together with the slipknot, being careful not to twist sts.
Work in K1, P1 Ribbing for 7 rnds.
On next rnd, place 7 RM as follows:
Next Rnd: Cont in K1, P1 Ribbing, work 6 sts, PRM, work 17 (19, 23, 25, 27, 29) sts for right sleeve, PRM, work 6 sts, PRM, work 62 (66, 74, 78, 82, 86) sts for front, PRM, work 6 sts, PRM, work 17 (19, 23, 25, 27, 29) sts for left sleeve, PRM, work 6 sts, PRM, work 62 (66, 74, 78, 82, 86) sts for back.

With larger needle, place 20 CM as follows:
Set-Up Rnd: *P1, K4, P1 (this will be Cable C chart), SRM, P1 (2, 4, 5, 6, 7) sts, PCM, P2, K2, P7, K2, P2, (this will be Cable B), PCM, P1 (2, 4, 5, 6, 7) sts, SRM, P1, K4, P1 (this will be Cable C), SRM, P3, K2, P2 (this will be Raglan 1), PCM, P1 (2, 4, 5, 6, 7) sts, PCM, P1, K4, P1 (this will be Cable C), PCM, P1 (2, 4, 5, 6, 7) sts, PCM, (P2, K2) twice, P3, K2, P6, K2, P3, (K2, P2) twice (this will be Cable A), PCM, P1 (2, 4, 5, 6, 7) sts, PCM, P1, K4, P1 (this will be Cable C), PCM, P1 (2, 4, 5, 6, 7) sts, PCM, P2, K2, P3 (this will be Raglan 2), SRM; rep from * once.
Work Set-Up Rnd once more, slipping all markers.

Begin working from Cables A, B, and C, Raglan 1 and 2 and Sleeve Chart as indicated below:
Rnd 1: *work Cable C chart, SRM, work Sleeve chart, SRM, work Cable C chart, SRM, work Raglan 1 chart, SCM, P1 (2, 4, 5, 6, 7) sts, SCM, work Cable C chart, SCM, P1 (2, 4, 5, 6, 7) sts, SCM, work Cable A chart, SCM, P1 (2, 4, 5, 6, 7) sts, SCM, work Cable C chart, SCM, P1 (2, 4, 5, 6, 7) sts, SCM, work Raglan 2 chart, SRM; rep from * once

Work through Rnd 16 of Raglan 1 and Raglan 2 charts. 64 sts inc. 246 (258, 282, 294, 306, 318) sts.

The Sleeve and Raglan charts are now complete. Continue all other cables as established, and work the following rnd:

Next Rnd: *Cable C, SRM, LI P-wise, P2, PCM, Cable C, SCM, P1 (2, 4, 5, 6, 7), SCM, Cable B, SCM, P1 (2, 4, 5, 6, 7), SCM, Cable C, SCM, P2, LI P-wise, SRM, Cable C, SRM, LI P-wise, P1, SCM, work Rnd 1 of Cable B, SCM, work in pattern across next 7 CMs, work Rnd 1 of Cable B, SCM, LI P-wise, SRM; rep from * once. 8 sts inc. 254 (266, 290, 302, 314, 326) sts.

Raglan Inc Rnd: *Work in pattern to first/next RM, SRM, LI as indicated, work to next RM, LI as indicated, SRM, work to next RM, SRM, LI as indicated, work to next RM, LI as indicated, SRM; rep from * once. 8 sts inc.

Cont in cable patterns as established while working a Raglan Inc Rnd 15 (20, 23, 26, 31, 37) more times, adding new sts as follows:
Sleeves: LI P-wise 4 (5, 7, 8, 9, 10) times each edge, then LI K-wise until all inc's are complete.
Front and Back: LI P-wise 0 (1, 3, 4, 5, 6) times, PCM, LI P-wise once, LI K-wise 4 times, LI P-wise once (Cable C), PCM, LI P-wise 1 (2, 2, 2, 6, 5) times, the LI K-wise until all inc's are complete.

Once all inc's are complete, there are 374 (426, 474, 510, 562, 622) sts in rnd, with each sleeve having 65 (77, 87, 95, 107, 121) sts and each front and back having 110 (124, 138, 148, 162, 178) sts, plus the 6-st Cable C divisions.

Separation Rnd: Cont in pattern, removing RMs and maintaining CMs as they are encountered, work to first RM, and place next 65 (77, 87, 95, 107, 121) sts on scrap yarn for right sleeve, noting chart rnd number. Using the Backward Loop method, CO 10 (10, 10, 14, 14, 14) sts at underarm. Work in pattern over next 122 (136, 150, 160, 174, 190) sts for the front. Place next 65 (77, 87, 95, 107, 121) sts on scrap yarn for left sleeve. Using the Backward Loop method, CO 10 (10, 10, 14, 14, 14) sts at underarm. Work in pattern over next 122 (136, 150, 160, 174, 190) sts for the back. Work in St st to the center of the CO sts at right underarm and place distinctive M for beginning of the rnd. 264 (292, 320, 348, 376, 408) sts.

Cont in pattern as established until work measures 12.25 (12.5, 13, 14, 14.25, 14.5)", or desired length from underarm less 1". Cont on larger needles by working 1" in K1, P1 Ribbing. Bind off loosely in rib.

Sleeves (make 2 the same)

With larger needle, PU 65 (77, 87, 95, 107, 121) sts held for right sleeve. PU and K 11 (11, 11, 15, 15, 15) sts at underarm placing distinctive M after 5 (5, 5, 7, 7, 7)th st as beginning of rnd. 76 (88, 98, 110, 122, 136) sts.

Work 2 rnds in pattern as established, then work the following Dec Rnd 8 (12, 15, 20, 22, 29) times every 18 (12, 10, 8, 7, 5)th rnd until there are 60 (64, 68, 70, 78, 78) sts.
Dec Rnd: K1, K2tog, work in pattern to last 3 sts, SSK, K1. 2 sts dec.

Work even in pattern until sleeve measures 18.5 (19, 19, 19.5, 20, 20)" from underarm or desired length allowing for 1" ribbing. Cont on larger needles by working 1" in K1, P1 ribbing.
Bind off loosely in rib.

Finishing

Weave in ends, wash and block to diagram.

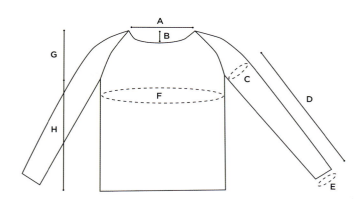

A 8.5 (9.5 10.5 11.25 11.5 13.25)"
B 1.25 (1.5, 1.5, 1.75, 2.25, 2.5)"
C 11.25 (13, 14.75, 16.5, 18.25, 20.5)"
D 18.5 (19, 19, 19.5, 20, 20)"
E 9 (9.5, 10, 11, 11, 11)"
F 35.75 (40.25, 44.5, 48.75, 53, 58)"
G 4.75 (5.25, 5.5, 6, 6.5, 7)"
H 12.25 (12.5, 13, 14, 14.25, 14.5)"

Cable A

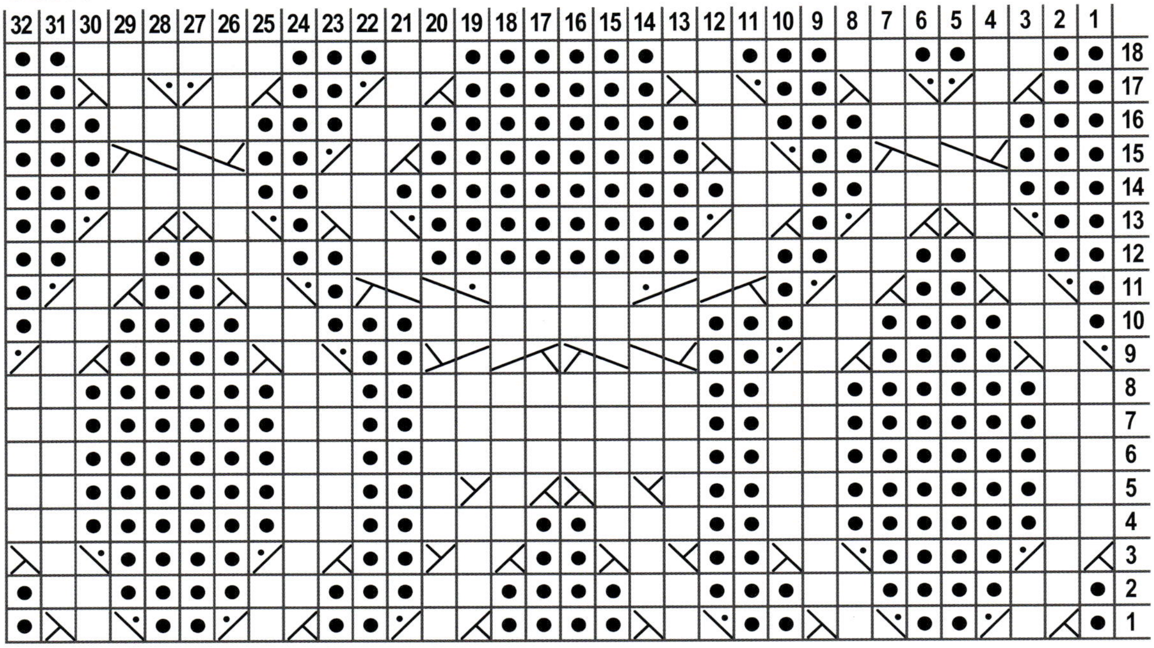

Legend:

- ☐ **knit** — knit stitch
- • **purl** — purl stitch
- ▪ **no stitch**
- ☐ **purl rep to size** [P1 (2, 4, 5, 6, 7) sts]
- L· **Lifted Increase P-wise** — Lift the st from the row below the first st on the left needle, placing on the left needle. Purl the lifed stitch.
- L **Lifted Increase K-wise** — Lift the st from the row below the first st on the left needle, placing on the left needle. Knit the stitch.
- **c2 over 1 left** — sl2 to CN, hold in front. k1, k2 from CN
- **c2 over 1 right** — sl1 to CN, hold in back. k2, k1 from CN
- **c2 over 1 left P** — sl2 to CN, hold in front. p1, k2 from CN
- **c2 over 1 right P** — sl1 to CN, hold in back. k2, p1 from CN
- **c2 over 2 left** — sl 2 to CN, hold in front. k2, k2 from CN
- **c2 over 2 right** — sl2 to CN, hold in back. k2, k2 from CN
- **c2 over 2 left P** — sl 2 to CN, hold in front. p2, k2 from CN
- **c2 over 2 right P** — sl2 to CN, hold in back. k2, p2 from CN
- **c2 over 3 right** — sl3 to CN, hold in back. k2, then k3 from CN

36 Sestina Pullover

Cable B

Cable C

Sestina Pullover

Raglan 1

Raglan 2

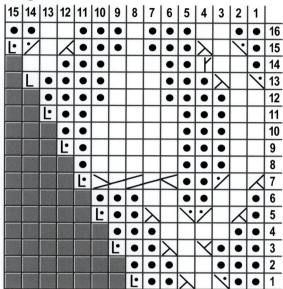

Sleeve Chart

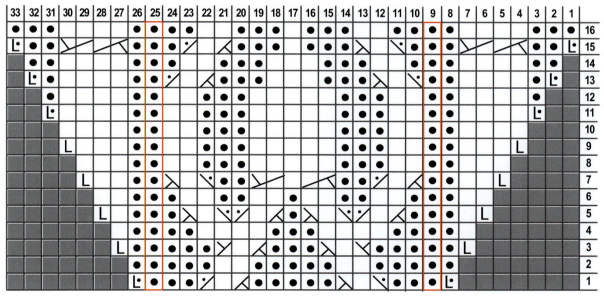

MACASKILL SCARF

by Sarah Dawn

FINISHED MEASUREMENTS
13.5 x 55" not including optional fringe.

YARN
Knit Picks Wool of the Andes Superwash Bulky (100% Superwash Wool, 137 yards/100g): Marble Heather 26512, 4 skeins

NEEDLES
US 10.75 (7mm) straight or circular needles, or size to obtain gauge

NOTIONS
Yarn Needle, 2 Cable Needles, Size K Crochet Hook for Fringe, optional.

GAUGE
15 sts and 17 rows = 4" in Scarf Cable Pattern, blocked (gauge for this project is approximate, changes will affect the amount of yarn used and the size.)

For pattern support, contact sarahdawnsdesigns@gmail.com

MacAskill Scarf

Notes:
This Giant Cable Scarf was designed to keep you warm. It's big enough that it can reach your ears if it's wrapped around your neck, it can be a hood if it's wrapped around your head; and, it's bulky enough to keep you warm even in the depths of winter. And, since it is knit in bulky-weight yarn, it doesn't take long to knit up! Customizable length lets you make it as long or short as you like, and optional fringe lets you dress it up as you desire.

This Scarf is one large cable repeat with a Seed Stitch Border. The cable repeat is done 5 times vertically, but can be repeated more times to lengthen the scarf if desired. Optional fringe is added using a crochet hook.

The scarf is fully charted and has full written instructions. Follow chart from right to left on RS rows (odd numbers) and left to right on WS rows (even numbers).

Knit Front, Back, Front (KFBF): Knit into the front, back and front of the st. 2 sts inc.
2/1 Right Purl Cross (2/1 RPC): Sl1 to CN, hold in back, K2, P1 from CN.
2/2 Right Purl Cross (2/2 RPC): Sl2 to CN, hold in back, K2, P2 from CN.
2/2 Right Cross (2/2 RC): Sl2 to CN, hold in back, K2, K2 from CN.
2/1/2 Right Purl Cross: (2/1/2 RPC): Sl2 to first CN, hold in back. Sl1 to 2nd CN, hold behind first CN, K2, bring first CN to front, P1 from 2nd CN, K2 from first CN.
2/1 Left Purl Cross (2/1 LPC): Sl2 to CN, hold in front, P1, K2 from CN.
2/2 Left Purl Cross (2/2 LPC): Sl2 to CN, hold in front, P2, K2, from CN.
2/2 Left Cross (2/2 LC): Sl2 to CN, hold in front, K2, K2 from CN.
2/1/2 Left Purl Cross (2/1/2 LPC): Sl2 to first CN, hold in front, Sl1 to 2nd CN, hold in back, K2, P1 from 2nd CN, K2 from first CN.
Dec over 5 sts (Dec5): Sl sts P-wise WYIB. Sl3 sts to RH needle, *pass 2nd st on RH needle over and off needle, Sl1 to LH needle, pass 2nd st on LH needle over and off needle*, Sl1 to RH needle; repeat from * to * once more, K1. 4 sts dec.

Scarf Cable Chart Written Instructions (worked flat)
Row 1 (RS): (K1, P1) to end of row.
Row 2 (WS): (P1, K1) to end of row.
Rows 3 and 4: Rep Rows 1 and 2
Row 5: K1, P1, K1, P3, K2, P11, K4, P11, K2, P2, (K1, P1) 2 times.
Row 6: P1, K1, P1, K3, P2, K11, P4, K11, P2, K2, (P1, K1) 2 times.
Row 7: (K1, P1) 2 times, P2, 2/1 LPC, P6, KFBF, P3, 2/2 LC, P3, KFBF, P6, 2/1 RPC, P2, (K1, P1) 2 times. 46 sts
Row 8: (P1, K1) 2 times, K3, P2, K6, P1, (P1, YO, P1) in 1 st, P1, K3, P4, K3, P1, (P1, YO, P1) in 1 st, P1, K6, P2, K3, (P1, K1) 2 times. 50 sts.
Row 9: (K1, P1) 2 times, P3, 2/1 LPC, P3, 2/2 RPC, P1, 2/1 LPC, P2, K4, P2, 2/1 RPC, P1, 2/2 LPC, P3, 2/1 RPC, P3, (K1, P1) 2 times.
Row 10: (P1, K1) 2 times, K4, P2, K3, P2, K4, P2, K2, P4, K2, P2, K4, P2, K3, P2, K4, (P1, K1) 2 times.
Row 11: (K1, P1) 2 times, P4, 2/1 LPC, 2/2 RPC, P3, 2/1 RPC, P2, 2/2 LC, P2, 2/1 LPC, P3, 2/2 LPC, 2/1 RPC, P4, (K1, P1) 2 times.
Row 12: (P1, K1) 2 times, K5, P4, K5, P2, K3, P4, K3, P2, K5, P4, K5, (P1, K1) 2 times.
Row 13: (K1, P1) 2 times, P5, 2/2 LC, P4, 2/1 RPC, P3, K4, P3, 2/1 LPC, P4, 2/2 RC, P5, (K1, P1) 2 times.
Row 14: (P1, K1) 2 times, K5, (P4, K4, P2, K4) 2 times, P4, K5, (P1, K1) 2 times.
Row 15: (K1, P1) 2 times, P4, 2/1 RPC, 2/2 LPC, P1, 2/1 RPC, P3, 2/1 RPC, 2/1 LPC, P3, 2/1 LPC, P1, 2/2 RPC, 2/1 LPC, P4, (K1, P1) 2 times.
Row 16: (P1, K1) 2 times, K4, P2, K3, P2, K1, P2, K4, P2, K2, P2, K4, P2, K1, P2, K3, P2, K4, (P1, K1) 2 times.
Row 17: (K1, P1) 2 times, P3, 2/1 RPC, P3, 2/1/2 RPC, P3, 2/1 RPC, P2, 2/1 LPC, P3, 2/1/2 LPC, P3, 2/1 LPC, P3, (K1, P1) 2 times.
Row 18: (P1, K1) 2 times, K3, P2, K4, P2, K1, P2, K3, P2, K4, P2, K3, P2, K1, P2, K4, P2, K3, (P1, K1) 2 times.
Row 19: (K1, P1) 2 times, P2, 2/1 RPC, P3, 2/1 RPC, P1, 2/2 LPC, 2/1 RPC, P4, 2/1 LPC, 2/2 RPC, P1, 2/1 LPC, P3, 2/1 LPC, P2, (K1, P1) 2 times.
Row 20: (P1, K1) 2 times, K2, (P2, K4) 2 times, P4, K6, P4, (K4, P2) 2 times, K2, (P1, K1) 2 times.
Row 21: (K1, P1) 2 times, P2, K2, P3, 2/1 RPC, P4, 2/2 LC, P6, 2/2 RC, P4, 2/1 LPC, P3, K2, P2, (K1, P1) 2 times.
Row 22: (P1, K1) 2 times, K2, P2, K3, P2, K5, P4, K6, P4, K5, P2, K3, P2, K2, (P1, K1) 2 times.
Row 23: (K1, P1) 2 times, P2, K2, P2, 2/1 LPC, P3, 2/2 RPC, 2/1 LPC, P4, 2/1 RPC, 2/2 LPC, P3, 2/1 RPC, P2, K2, P2, (K1, P1) 2 times.
Row 24: (P1, K1) 2 times, K2, P2, K2, (P2, K4, P2, K3) 2 times, P2, K4, (P2, K2) 2 times, (P1, K1) 2 times.
Row 25: (K1, P1) 2 times, P2, K2, P2, 2/1 LPC, P1, 2/2 RPC, P3, 2/1 LPC, P2, 2/1 RPC, P3, 2/2 LPC, P1, 2/1 RPC, P2, K2, P2, (K1, P1) 2 times.
Row 26: (P1, K1) 2 times, K2, P2, K3, P2, K1, P2, K6, P2, K2, P2, K6, P2, K1, P2, K3, P2, K2, (P1, K1) 2 times.
Row 27: (K1, P1) 2 times, P2, K2, P3, Dec5, P6, 2/1 LPC, 2/1 RPC, P6, Dec5, P3, K2, P2, (K1, P1) 2 times. 42 sts
Row 28: (P1, K1) 2 times, K2, P2, K11, P4, K11, P2, K2, (P1, K1) 2 times.
Row 29: (K1, P1) 2 times, P2, K2, P3, KFBF, P6, 2/1 RPC, 2/1 LPC, P6, KFBF, P3, K2, P2, (K1, P1) 2 times. 46 sts
Row 30: (P1, K1) 2 times, K2, P2, K3, P1, (P1, YO, P1) in 1 st, P1, K6, P2, K2, P2, K6, P1, (P1, YO, P1) in 1 st, P1, K3, P2, K2, (P1, K1) 2 times. 50 sts
Row 31: (K1, P1) 2 times, P2, K2, P2, 2/1 RPC, P1, 2/2 LPC, P3, 2/1 RPC, P2, 2/1 LPC, P3, 2/2 RPC, P1, 2/1 LPC, P2, K2, P2, (K1, P1) 2 times.
Row 32: Rep Row 24.
Row 33: (K1, P1) 2 times, P2, K2, P2, 2/1 LPC, P3, 2/2 LPC, 2/1 RPC, P4, 2/1 LPC, 2/2 RPC, P3, 2/1 RPC, P2, K2, P2, (K1, P1) 2 times.
Row 34: Rep Row 22.
Row 35: (K1, P1) 2 times, P2, K2, P3, 2/1 LPC, P4, 2/2 LC, P6, 2/2 RC, P4, 2/1 RPC, P3, K2, P2, (K1, P1) 2 times.

Row 36: Rep Row 20.
Row 37: (K1, P1) 2 times, P2, 2/1 LPC, P3, 2/1 LPC, P1, 2/2 RPC, 2/1 LPC, P4, 2/1 RPC, 2/2 LPC, P1, 2/1 RPC, P3, 2/1 RPC, P2, (K1, P1) 2 times.
Row 38: Rep Row 18.
Row 39: (K1, P1) 2 times, P3, 2/1 LPC, P3, 2/1/2 RPC, P3, 2/1 LPC, P2, 2/1 RPC, P3, 2/1/2 LPC, P3, 2/1 RPC, P3, (K1, P1) 2 times.
Row 40: Rep Row 16.
Row 41: (K1, P1) 2 times, P4, 2/1 LPC, 2/2 RPC, P1, 2/1 LPC, P3, 2/1 LPC, 2/1 RPC, P3, 2/1 RPC, P1, 2/2 LPC, 2/1 RPC, P4, (K1, P1) 2 times.
Row 42: Rep Row 14.
Row 43: (K1, P1) 2 times, P5, 2/2 LC, P4, 2/1 LPC, P3, K4, P3, 2/1 RPC, P4, 2/2 RC, P5, (K1, P1) 2 times.
Row 44: Rep Row 12.
Row 45: (K1, P1) 2 times, P4, 2/1 RPC, 2/2 LPC, P3, 2/1 LPC, P2, 2/2 LC, P2, 2/1 RPC, P3, 2/2 RPC, 2/1 LPC, P4, (K1, P1) 2 times.
Row 46: Rep Row 10.
Row 47: (K1, P1) 2 times, P3, 2/1 RPC, P3, 2/2 LPC, P1, 2/1 RPC, P2, K4, P2, 2/1 LPC, P1, 2/2 RPC, P3, 2/1 LPC, P3, (K1, P1) 2 times.
Row 48: (P1, K1) 2 times, K3, P2, K6, P2, K1, P2, K3, P4, K3, P2, K1, P2, K6, P2, K3, (P1, K1) 2 times.
Row 49: (K1, P1) 2 times, P2, 2/1 RPC, P6, Dec5, P3, 2/2 LC, P3, Dec5, P6, 2/1 LPC, P2, (K1, P1) 2 times. 42 sts.
Row 50: Rep Row 6.
Rows 51 to 54: Rep Rows 1 and 2 two times.

Body:

Cast on 42 sts. Work Scarf Cable from chart or written instructions as follows:
Work Rows 1-50 of the Scarf Cable Chart.
Rep Rows 7-50 of the Scarf Cable Chart 4 more times (5 times in total).
Work Rows 51 to 54 of the Scarf Cable Chart.

BO all sts. Cut yarn and draw through last st.

Finishing

Weave in ends. Wash, and block to desired dimensions.

Optional Fringe
Cut 80 6" pieces of yarn (or, double the length you want your fringe to be). Fold pieces in half.
Place scarf RS facing up.
Using crochet hook, *insert hook from bottom to top of work, through loop of CO edge. Place loop of folded yarn piece in hook and pull through the CO loop.
Take ends of cut yarn and pull through loop on crochet hook. Ends of yarn should be as even as possible.
Pull to tighten up.
Repeat from *for remainder of CO edge.
Repeat for BO edge.

Trim fringe if necessary.

Scarf Cable Chart

Legend:

- ▢ **knit**
  RS: knit stitch
  WS: purl stitch
- ⊙ **purl**
  RS: purl stitch
  WS: knit stitch
- ■ **no stitch**
- Ⅴ **KFBF**
  Knit into the front, back and front of the st
- △ **k5tog**
  Decrease 5 stitches
- ⊡ **(P1, YO, P1) in 1 st**
  WS: (P1, YO, P1) all in 1 st to make 3 STS from 1
- ▢ **pattern repeat**

- **2/1 right purl cross**
  SL1 to CN, hold in back. K2, P1 from CN
- **2/1 left purl cross**
  SL2 to CN, hold in front. P1, K2 from CN
- **2/2 right purl cross**
  SL2 to CN, hold in back. K2, P2 from CN
- **2/2 left purl cross**
  SL2 to CN, hold in front. P2, K2 from CN
- **2/2 right cross**
  SL2 to CN, hold in back. K2, K2 from CN
- **c2 over 2 left**
  SL2 to CN, hold in front. K2, K2 from CN
- **2/1/2 left purl cross**
  SL2 to first CN, hold in front. SL1 to 2nd CN, hold in back, K2, P1 from 2nd CN, K2 from first CN.
- **2/1/2 right purl cross**
  SL2 to first CN, hold in back. SL1 to 2nd CN, hold behind first CN, K2, bring first CN to front, P1 from 2nd CN, K2 from first CN.

DIAMOND LATTICE PULLOVER

by Kephren Pritchett

FINISHED MEASUREMENTS
33 (36.5, 41, 44.5, 49, 52.5, 57, 61.25, 65)" finished bust measurement, garment is meant to be worn with 1 to 3" of positive ease

YARN
Knit Picks Wool of the Andes Worsted (100% Peruvian Highland Wool; 110 yards/50g): Opal Heather 25645, 9 (9, 10, 12, 13, 14, 15, 17, 18) skeins

NEEDLES
US 6 (4mm) 24" or 32" circular needle plus DPNs or 32" or longer circular needle for Magic Loop technique, or size to obtain gauge
US 7 (4.5mm) 24" or 32" circular needle plus DPNs or 32" or longer circular needle for Magic Loop technique, or size to obtain gauge

NOTIONS
Yarn Needle, Stitch Markers, Cable Needle, Scrap Yarn or Stitch Holders, Spare DPNs

GAUGE
18 sts and 24 rnds = 4" in Rev St st in the rnd on larger needles, blocked
18 sts and 24 rnds = 4" over Diamond Lattice Chart in the rnd on larger needles, blocked
22 sts and 24 rnds = 4" over Argyll Chart in the rnd on larger needles, blocked
20 sts = 4" in K2, P2 Rib in the rnd on smaller needles, blocked
18 sts = 4" in K1, P1 Rib in the rnd on smaller needles, blocked

For pattern support, contact kephrenknittingstudio@gmail.com

Diamond Lattice Pullover

Notes:
The sleeves are cast on at the cuffs and worked in the round to the underarms, where the underarm stitches are set aside and the remaining sleeve stitches are placed on holders. The body is cast on at the ribbed hem and worked in the cable pattern to the underarms, where underarm stitches are placed on holders and the sleeves are joined. The yoke is worked in rounds and shaped with raglan decreases. The raglan seamlines are worked in Stockinette stitch on a reverse Stockinette background. At the top of the yoke, front neck stitches are bound off and the back and shoulders are worked flat to shape the crew neck. The remaining stitches are bound off to create a ridge to attach the folded collar. Stitches are picked up around the neck opening and worked in ribbing to create the collar, then folded to the inside and attached to the pick-up row. The underarms are joined invisibly with Kitchener stitch.

Cable patterns are provided in chart form only. Begin working cable patterns on Row 1 unless otherwise noted. In the Raglan Shaping section, when there are no longer enough stitches to work the cable patterns, work the stitches as they appear (knit the knit stitches and purl the purl stitches.) Charts are worked in the round to the front neck bind off, then worked flat for the remaining rows of the neck shaping. Odd-numbered rows are worked on the WS and even-numbered rows are worked on the RS.

K2, P2 Rib (in the rnd over a multiple of 4 sts)
Rnd 1: *K2, P2; rep from * to end of rnd.
Rep Rnd 1 for pattern.

K1, P1 Rib (in the rnd over an even number of sts)
Rnd 1: *K1, P1; rep from * to end of rnd.
Rep Rnd 1 for pattern.

Make 1 Right Purl-wise (M1R P-wise): With left needle, lift the yarn between the needles from the back, purl into the front of this loop.

Make 1 Left Purl-wise (M1L P-wise): With left needle, lift the yarn between the needles from the front, purl into the back of this loop.

Special Bind-off
The folded collar is attached to the pick-up row using a variation of Kitchener stitch; live sts on the needle are joined to the bind off ridge at the base of the collar using a yarn needle.

DIRECTIONS

Sleeves
The sleeves are worked in rnds beginning at the cuffs.

Cuffs
With smaller DPNs or smaller, longer circular needle for Magic Loop, using the Cable Cast On method CO 48 (48, 52, 56, 60, 60, 60, 64) sts. PM and join to work in the rnd, being careful not to twist sts.

Work in K2, P2 Rib until piece measures 3". P 1 rnd. Change to larger needle.
Setup Cable Pattern: P4 (4, 10, 10, 14, 14, 18, 22, 24), PM, P11 (11, 10, 12, 12, 12, 10, 8, 9), work Argyll Chart over next 22 sts, P11 (11, 10, 12, 12, 12, 10, 8, 9).
Inc Rnd: P to M, SM, M1L P-wise, work in pattern to end, M1R P-wise. 2 sts inc.
Work as established, repeating Inc Rnd every 19 (20, 17, 17, 15, 13, 7, 5, 5)th rnd 4 (4, 5, 5, 6, 7, 14, 18, 18) more times. 58 (58, 64, 68, 74, 76, 90, 98, 102) sts.
WE until sleeve measures 19 (19.5, 19.5, 20, 20, 20.5, 20.5, 21, 21)" ending with an even-numbered row of Argyll Pattern.
Prepare to join sleeves to body: Remove M, place next 4 (4, 10, 10, 14, 14, 18, 22, 24) sts on a holder for underarm, remove M, place remaining 54 (54, 54, 58, 60, 62, 72, 76, 78) sts on a separate holder or spare needle. Set aside.

Body
Hem
With smaller circular needle and using the Cable Cast On method, CO 164 (180, 200, 216, 236, 252, 272, 292, 308) sts. PM, and join to work in the rnd, being careful not to twist sts. Work in K2, P2 Rib until piece measures 2". P 1 rnd. Change to larger needle.

Setup Cable Patterns: P1 (1, 3, 7, 10, 10, 13, 16, 15) work Row 17 of Argyll Chart over next 22 sts, work Diamond Lattice Chart over next 32 (40, 40, 40, 40, 48, 48, 48, 56) sts, work Row 17 of Argyll Chart over next 22 sts, P6 (6, 16, 24, 34, 34, 44, 54, 54), work Row 17 of Argyll Chart over next 22 sts, work Diamond Lattice Chart over next 32 (40, 40, 40, 40, 48, 48, 48, 56) sts, work Row 17 of Argyll Chart over next 22 sts, P5 (5, 13, 17, 24, 24, 31, 38, 39).
WE as established until body measures 14 (14.5, 14.5, 15, 15, 15.5, 15.5, 16, 16)" ending with the same row of Argyll Chart as sleeves.

Raglan Shaping
Join Sleeves to Body: K1, work next 76 (84, 88, 96, 102, 110, 116, 122, 128) sts in pattern for Front, K1, PM, place next 4 (4, 10, 10, 14, 14, 18, 22, 24) sts on a holder for underarm, attach first set of held sleeve sts and K1, work next 52 (52, 52, 56, 58, 60, 70, 74, 76) sleeve sts in pattern, K1, PM, K1, work 76 (84, 88, 96, 102, 110, 116, 122, 128) sts in pattern for Back, K1, PM, place next 4 (4, 10, 10, 14, 14, 18, 22, 24) sts on a holder for underarm, attach second held sleeve sts and K1, work 52 (52, 52, 56, 58, 60, 70, 74, 76) sleeve sts in pattern, K1, PM for beginning of rnd. 264 (280, 288, 312, 328, 348, 380, 400, 416) sts.

Sizes 33, 36.5, 57, 61.25, and 65" Only
Raglan Dec Rnd: *SSK, work in pattern to 2 sts before M, K2tog, SM; rep from * 3 more times. 8 sts dec.
Sleeve Dec Rnd: *Work in pattern to M, SM, SSK, work in pattern to 2 sts before M, K2tog, SM; rep from * 1 more time. 4 sts dec.

Rep these 2 rnds 3 (2, -, -, -, -, 2, 2, 2) more times. 38 (42, -, -, -, -, -, 60, 64, 66) sts each sleeve, 70 (80, -, -, -, -, 112, 118, 124) sts each front and back. 216 (244, -, -, -, -, 344, 364, 380) total sts.

All Sizes
Raglan Dec Rnd: *SSK, work in pattern to 2 sts before M, K2tog, SM; rep from * 3 more times. 8 sts dec.
Next Rnd: WE in pattern.
Rep these 2 rnds 9 (11, 16, 18, 19, 20, 19, 21, 22) more times. 18 (18, 20, 20, 20, 20, 20, 20, 20) sts each sleeve, 50 (56, 56, 60, 64, 70, 72, 74, 78) sts each front and back. 136 (148, 152, 160, 168, 180, 184, 188, 196) total sts.

Front Neck BO: SSK, work 14 (14, 14, 14, 16, 19, 19, 19, 20) sts in pattern, BO center 18 (24, 24, 28, 28, 28, 30, 32, 34) sts for front neck, *work in pattern to 2 sts before M, K2tog, SM, SSK; rep from * 2 more times, work in pattern to 2 sts before end of rnd M, K2tog, work sts as they appear to front neck BO turn to begin working flat. 110 (116, 120, 124, 132, 144, 146, 148, 154) total sts, 15 (15, 15, 15, 17, 20, 20, 20, 21) each Front, 48 (54, 54, 58, 62, 68, 70, 72, 76) for Back, 16 (16, 18, 18, 18, 18, 18, 18, 18) each Sleeve.
Next Row (WS): WE in pattern.

Sizes 33 (36.5, 41, 44.5, 49)" Only
Raglan and Neck Dec Row (RS): K1, SSK, *work in pattern to 2 sts before M, K2tog, SM, SSK; rep from * 3 more times, work in pattern to last 3 sts, K2tog, K1. 10 sts dec.
Next Row (WS): WE in pattern.
Rep these 2 rows 4 (4, 4, 4, 2, -, -, -, -) more times. 6 (6, 8, 8, 12, -, -, -, -) sts each sleeve, 38 (44, 44, 48, 56, -, -, -, -) back neck sts, 5 (5, 5, 5, 11, -, -, -, -) sts each side of front neck. 60 (66, 70, 74, 102, -, -, -, -) total sts.

Sizes 49, 52.5, 57, 61.25, and 65" Only
Raglan and Neck Dec Row (RS): K1, SSK, *work in pattern to 2 sts before M, K2tog, SM, SSK; rep from * 3 more times, work in pattern to last 3 sts, K2tog, K1. 10 sts dec.
Fronts and Back Raglan Dec Row (WS): *Work in pattern to 2 sts before M, SSP, SM, work in pattern to M, SM, P2tog; rep from * once more, work in pattern to end. 4 sts dec.
Rep these 2 rows - (-, -, -, 1, 4, 4, 4, 4) more times. - (-, -, -, 8, 8, 8, 8, 8) sts each sleeve, - (-, -, -, 48, 48, 50, 52, 56) back neck sts, - (-, -, -, 5, 5, 5, 5, 6) sts each side of front neck. - (-, -, -, 74, 74, 76, 78, 84) total sts.

All Sizes
BO all sts in pattern.

Neck Band
Change to smaller needle and beginning at left front shoulder, PU and K 11 sts from shaped neck edge, 18 (24, 24, 28, 28, 28, 30, 32, 34) sts from Front Neck BO, 11 sts from shaped neck edge, 6 (6, 8, 8, 8, 8, 8, 8, 8) sts from top of Right sleeve, 38 (44, 44, 48, 48, 48, 50, 52, 54) Back sts, 6 (6, 8, 8, 8, 8, 8, 8, 8) sts from top of Left Sleeve. 90 (102, 106, 114, 114, 114, 118, 122, 126) sts. PM and join in the rnd. Purl 1 row. Work in K1, P1 Rib until neck band measures 2". Break rnd yarn leaving a long tail and thread onto a yarn needle. Fold neck band to WS and attach live sts to the PU row using Kitchener st.

Finishing
Turn the sweater inside out. Return held body and sleeve underarm sts to larger circular needle or 2 DPNs and PU 1 additional st each side. Cut a length of yarn about 24" long and thread onto a yarn needle. Join underarm sts with Kitchener st.

Weave in ends, wash and block to schematic measurements.

Legend:

- ⊡ **purl** — purl stitch
- ☐ **knit** — knit stitch
- ▭ **repeat pattern**
- **Right Twist purl BG** — SL1 to CN, hold in back. K1, P1 from CN
- **Left Twist purl BG** — SL1 to CN, hold in front. P1. K1 from CN
- **Left Twist** — SL1 to CN, hold in front. K1, K1 from CN
- **Right Twist** — Sl1 to CN, hold in back. K1, K1 from CN
- **c2over 1 left P** — SL2 to CN, hold in front. P1, K2 from CN
- **c2over 1 right P** — SL1 to CN, hold in back. K2, P1 from CN
- **c2over 1 right** — SL1 to CN, hold in back. K2, K1 from CN
- **c2 over 1 left** — SL2 to CN, hold in front. K1, K2 from CN
- **c2over 2 right** — SL2 to CN, hold in back. K2, K2 from CN
- **c2 over 2 left** — SL2 to CN, hold in front. K2, K2 from CN

Diamond Lattice Pullover

Diamond Lattice Chart

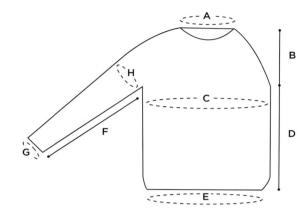

A 20 (22.75, 23.5, 25.25, 25.25, 25.25, 26.25, 27, 28)"
B 6.75 (7.25, 7.75, 8.5, 8.75, 9.25, 9.75, 10.5, 11)"
C 33 (36.5, 41, 44.5, 49, 52.5, 57, 61.25, 65)"
D 14 (14.5, 14.5, 15, 15, 15.5, 15.5, 16, 16)"
E 32.75 (36, 40, 43.25, 47.25, 50.5, 54.5, 58.5, 61.5)"
F 19 (19.5, 19.5, 20, 20, 20.5, 20.5, 21, 21)"
G 9.5 (9.5, 10.5, 11.25, 12, 12, 12, 12, 12.75)"
H 12 (12, 13.25, 14.25, 15.5, 16, 19, 21, 21.75)"

Argyll Chart

Diamond Lattice Pullover

WROUGHT IRON WRAP

by Margaret Mills

FINISHED MEASUREMENTS
18 (30)" x 60"

YARN
Knit Picks Wool of the Andes Worsted (100% Peruvian Highland Wool; 110 yards/50g): Rooibos Heather 25642, 11 (19) balls

NEEDLES
US 7 (4.5mm) 24" or longer circular needles, or size to obtain gauge

NOTIONS
Yarn Needle, 4 (6) Stitch Markers, Cable Needle

GAUGE
30 sts and 28 rows = 4" over Large Chart Rows 20-56, blocked

19 sts = 4" in Garter stitch, blocked (row gauge is not important)

Wrought Iron Wrap

Notes:

The Wrought Iron Wrap is a large, heavily cabled wrap. If you LOVE cables, and want to show that off while staying toasty warm, this wrap is for you! A narrow cable, with a complicated-looking but very manageable 32-row repeat, frames the large 64-row repeat panel reminiscent of fancy decorative ironwork. Narrow 1x1 twists separate the panels, and the edges are all worked in Garter stitch. There are two width options: the narrower size features one repeat of the Large chart panel and two repeats of the Small chart panel across the width; the wider size features two repeats of the Large chart panel and three repeats of the Small chart panel across the width.

The entire wrap is knit in one piece from cast on to bind off. When working the charts, read RS rows (even numbers) from right to left, and WS rows (odd numbers) from left to right.

Charts: Here is some explanation of the logic of the charts, to free you from having to look at them constantly. The cables are made up of compartments, each 9 sts wide and 8 rows long (separated by one st), and each compartment contains two 2-st cable strands. In the Small chart, there are two compartments across and four compartments along each repeat. At the beginning of each compartment (e.g., Small chart row 2), the two strands within each compartment are at the center of the compartment, crossing each other (e.g., sts 7-11 and sts 17-21). From that cross, the two strands have two options: they can either both stay in the center of the compartment and create a twist (e.g., Small chart rows 11-17, sts 7-11) or they can both move out from the center to the edges of the compartment and create a loop (e.g., Small chart rows 11-17, sts 15-23). A twist is never followed by another twist. When there are loops in neighboring compartments (e.g., Small chart rows 3-7), the loops cross where they meet (row 6 sts, 12-16). The same logic applies to the Large chart, which has five compartments across and eight compartments along each repeat, plus the framing strands along each side. If you follow this logic, you can limit your chart reading to the second RS row in each compartment.

DIRECTIONS

Wrap

CO 95 (161) sts. K 6 rows.

Setup Row (WS): K4, PM, follow Row 1 of Small chart over next 21 sts, PM, follow Row 1 of Large chart over next 45 sts, PM, follow Row 1 of Small chart over next 21 sts, PM, Narrow wrap only: K4 to end, Wide wrap only: follow Row 1 of Large chart over next 45 sts, PM, follow Row 1 of Small chart over next 21 sts, PM, K4. 109 (183) sts.

Continue to K the first 4 sts and last 4 sts of every row. Work from Large and Small charts as established through Row 9 of each chart.

Work from Large chart as established, repeating Rows 10-73 5 times, then work Rows 10-65 once, then work Rows 2-9 once, while at the same time working from Small chart as established, repeating Rows 10-41 12 times. Stitch count inc to 125 (216) sts on Rows 20-56 and Rows 68-72 of Large chart.

After completing described number of repeats, work from Small chart Row 42 and from Large chart Row 74. 95 (161) sts.

K 4 rows.
BO all sts.

Finishing

Weave in ends. Pin to measurements, then cover with a damp cloth. Leave until the covering cloth is entirely dry.

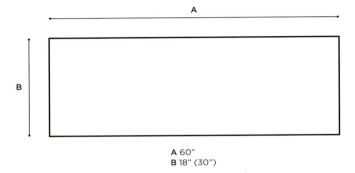

A 60"
B 18" (30")

Small Chart

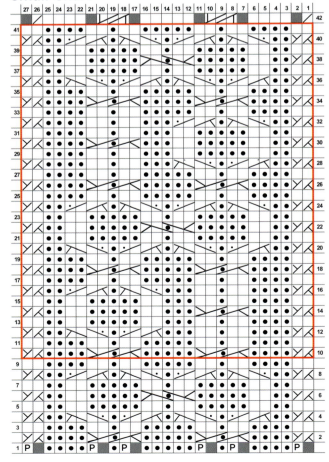

Legend:

- ⊡ **purl**
  RS: purl stitch
  WS: knit stitch

- ☐ **knit**
  RS: knit stitch
  WS: purl stitch

- ■ **no stitch**

- P **PFB**
  Purl into the front and the back of the stitch

- V **Central Double Inc**
  (K1tbl, K1) in one stitch, then insert left needle point behind the vertical strand that runs down between 2 sts just made, and K1tbl into this strand to make 3rd st of group.

- A **DEC5to1**
  SL3 to RH needle P-wise. SL next 2 sts to RH needle, one at a time, K-wise, then SL3 sts back to LH needle P-wise. *On LH needle, pass 2nd st over 1st and off needle. SL1 to RH needle. On RH needle, pass 2nd st over 1st and off needle. SL1 to LH needle. Rep from * once more. K1. 4 sts decreased.

- **P1 YO P1 in 1 st**
  (P1, YO, P1) all in 1 st to make 3 sts from 1

- **k2tog**
  Knit two stitches together as one stitch

- ▢ **pattern repeat**

- **C1 over 1 right**
  SL1 to CN, hold in back. K1 then K1 from CN

- **C2 over 1 right P**
  SL1 to CN, hold in back. K2, P1 from CN

- **C2 over 1 left P**
  SL2 to CN, hold in front. P1, K2 from CN

- **C2 over 2 right/dec**
  SL3 to CN, hold in back. K2TOG, then K1, K2TOG from CN

- **C2 over 2 left P**
  SL2 to CN, hold in front. P2, K2 from CN

- **C2 over 2 right P**
  SL2 to CN, hold in back. K2, P2 from CN

- **C2 over 2 left/purl bg**
  SL2 to CN, hold in front. K2, P1, then K2 from CN

- **C2 over 2 right/purl bg**
  SL3 to CN, hold in back. K2, then P1, K2 from CN

Large Chart

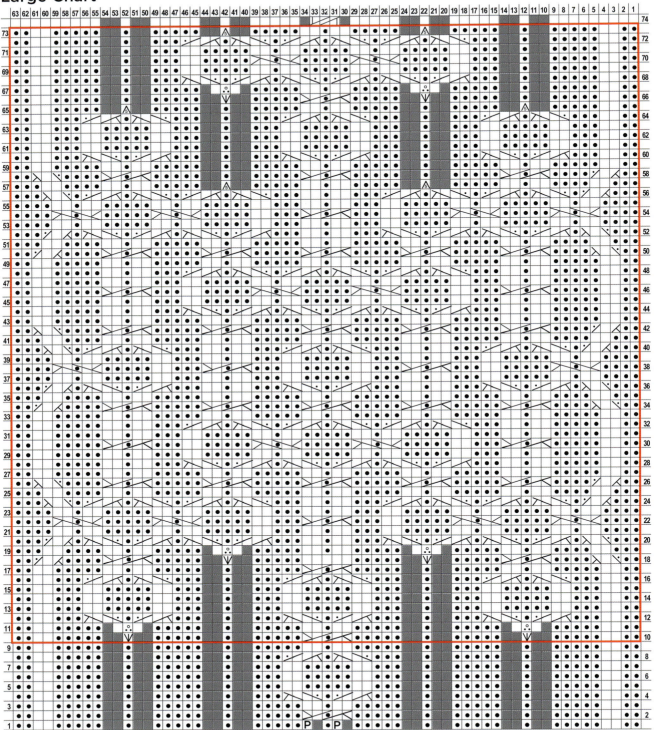

SIONANN CARDI

by Stephannie Tallent

FINISHED MEASUREMENTS
32 (36, 40, 44, 48, 52, 56)" finished bust measurement, buttoned; garment is meant to be worn with 3-4" of positive ease

YARN
Knit Picks Wool of the Andes Worsted Tweed (80% Peruvian Highland Wool, 20% Donegal Tweed; 110 yards/50g): Sequoia Heather 25448, 13 (14, 15, 17, 19, 20, 22) balls

NEEDLES
US 5 (3.75mm) straight or 32" circular needles for body, plus DPNs or two 24" circular needles for two circulars technique, or one 32" or longer circular needle for Magic Loop technique for sleeves, or size to obtain gauge

US 4 (3.5mm) DPNs or two 24" circular needles for two circulars technique, or one 32" or longer circular needle for Magic Loop technique for cuff ribbing, plus 32" circular needles for neckline ribbing and button band, or size to obtain gauge

NOTIONS
Yarn Needle, Stitch Markers, 2 Cable Needles, Scrap Yarn or Stitch Holders, 6 Buttons, amount is customizable

GAUGE
32 sts and 30 Rows = 4" in Cable Pattern (worked on Swatch Chart) on larger needles, blocked. The cable pattern is very stretchy.
22 sts and 30 Rows = 4" in Moss Stitch on larger needles, blocked. The cable pattern is very stretchy.

Sionann Cardi

Notes:

The sweater is knit from the top down, with stitches picked up from the saddle tabs, fronts and back joined at the armholes, and the garment continued in one piece.
The sleeves are worked by placing the live saddle tab stitches back on the needle and by picking up stitches along the armhole, working short rows for the cap shaping, then continuing in the round.

Waist shaping is easily modified, as decreases and increases occur in the Moss stitch panels adjacent to the cabled panels. Total length is also easily modified in the hem-to-armhole area by working longer prior to bust decreases, by working the waist longer, or by working longer after the hip increases. Pick up stitches more densely towards the neckline edge; the cabled motif has a tighter gauge than the seed stitch section.

Use the knitted cast on for all cast ons unless otherwise specified. If the cast on is charted, work the knitted cast on at the beginning of the row, and work the stitches to set up for the following row (knit or purl). Unless otherwise noted all knitted cast on stitches are to be immediately worked. I recommend working the original edge stitch through the back loop to tighten it.

Left back, left front, right back, and right front refer to the sweater as worn.

Note that some charts are specific for each size or set of sizes (Back Neck and Main Back charts). Work each named chart specific for your size.

The Small Main Chart is used for the saddle tab, sleeves, and front panels. Work it as shown for the right saddle strap, right sleeve, and right front. Work a 2/1/2 LCP rather than the charted 2/1/2 RCP for the left saddle strap, sleeve, and front (stitch highlighted in green on the charts). Although it is shown as flat knitting, work it in the round for the sleeves, working all rows as RS rows.

Charts for transitioning to ribbing after working Row 14 or 30 are included for the Back and Small Main Chart patterns. Conceal short row wraps as you come to them unless otherwise noted.

Slip markers as you reach them.

Work all increases and decreases to maintain Moss stitch pattern unless otherwise directed.

Read all pattern notes included at the beginning of each section.

Moss Stitch Pattern (worked flat over an even number of sts)
Row 1 (RS): (K1, P1) to end.
Row 2 (WS): (P1, K1) to end.
Row 3: (P1, K1) to end.
Row 4: (K1, P1) to end.

Rep Rows 1-4 for pattern.

Moss Stitch Pattern (worked flat over an odd number of sts)
Row 1 (RS): (K1, P1) to 1 st before end, K1.
Row 2 (WS): (K1, P1) to 1 st before end, K1.
Row 3: (P1, K1) to 1 st before end, P1.
Row 4: (P1, K1) to 1 st before end, P1.

Rep Rows 1-4 for pattern.

Moss Stitch Pattern (in the rnd over an even number of sts)
Rnds 1, 2: (K1, P1) to end.
Rnds 3, 4: (P1, K1) to end.

Rep Rnds 1-4 for pattern.

Moss Stitch Pattern (in the rnd over an odd number of sts)
Rnds 1, 2: (K1, P1) to 1 st before end, K1.
Rnds 3, 4: (P1, K1) to 1 st before end, P1.

Rep Rnds 1-4 for pattern.

2/1 LCP SSK: Sl 2 sts to CN and hold in front, P1, Sl sts back to LH needle, K1, SSK.
2/1 LCP: Sl 2 sts to CN and hold in front; P1; K2 from CN.
2/1 RCP K2tog: Sl 1 st to RH needle; Sl next st to CN and hold in back; Sl st from RH needle to LH needle; K2tog, K1, P1 from CN.
2/1 RCP: Sl 1 st to CN and hold in back; K2; P1 from CN.
2/1/2 LPC: Sl 2 sts to 1st CN and hold in front; Sl 1 st to 2nd CN and hold in back; K2; P1 from 2nd CN; K2 from 1st CN.
2/1/2 RPC: Sl 2 sts to 1st CN and hold in back; Sl 1 st to 2nd CN and hold in back; K2; P1 from 2nd CN; K2 from 1st CN.
2/2 LC: Sl 2 sts to CN and hold in front; K2; K2 from CN.
2/2 LCKP: Sl 2 sts to CN and hold in front; K1, P1; K2 from CN.
2/2 LCP: Sl 2 sts to CN and hold in front; P2; K2 from CN.
2/2 LCP2tog: Sl P st to RH needle, Sl 2 sts to CN and hold in front; Sl P st back to LH needle, P2tog, P1; K2 from CN.
2/2 RC: Sl 2 sts to CN and hold in back; K2; K2 from CN.
2/2 RCKP: Sl 2 sts to CN and hold in back; K2; K1, P1 from CN.
2/2 RCP: Sl 2 sts to CN and hold in back; K2; P2 from CN.
2/2 RCPK: Sl 2 sts to CN and hold in back; K2; P1, K1 from CN.
2/2 RCP2tog: Sl 2 sts to CN and hold in back; K2; P1 from CN, Sl last P st to LH needle, P2tog.
2/2 LCPK: Sl 2 sts to CN and hold in front; P1, K1; K2 from CN.

DIRECTIONS

Saddle Tab

Work one each Left and Right Saddle Tab using the Small Main Chart as follows below. Remember to work the 2/1/2 RCP as a 2/1/2 LCP for the left saddle strap.
Using larger needles, CO 35 sts.

Set Up Row (WS): Work Row 32 of chart.
Work Small Main Chart for 3 (3.25, 3.5, 3.5, 3.75, 3.75, 4)", ending having worked a WS Row (note Row for later reference). Place sts on scrap yarn.

Back

Orientate Saddle Tab CO sts towards the neck when picking up sts.

The uncharted sts on either side of the Main Back Chart are worked as RS: K1, Moss st to chart, work chart, Moss st to 1 st before end, K1. For WS: P1, Moss st to chart, work chart, Moss st to 1 st before end, P1. Maintain the knit columns and Moss stitch pattern as established until otherwise noted in the armhole shaping.

Right Back Shoulder

Refer to appropriate size Back Neck Chart, section outlined in blue.

With RS facing and live sts on left, CO sts to the right, PU and K 9 (9, 22, 22, 22, 30, 30) sts from edge of the Right Saddle Strap (Row 1 of Back Neck Chart, section outlined in blue), PM, then PU and K an additional 10 (12, 3, 4, 5, 2, 3) sts. 19 (21, 25, 26, 27, 32, 33) sts

Row 2 (WS): P1, work Moss st to M, work Row 2 of Back Neck Chart, section outlined in blue.

Row 3 (RS): Work Row 3 of Back Neck Chart, section outlined in blue.

Work through Row 6 of Back Neck Chart, section outlined in blue. Place sts on holder or scrap yarn.

Left Back Shoulder

Refer to appropriate size Back Neck Chart, section outlined in green.

With RS facing and live stitches on right, PU & K 10 (12, 3, 4, 5, 2, 3) sts from edge of the left saddle strap, PM, then PU and K an additional 9 (9, 22, 22, 22, 30, 30) sts (Row 1 of Chart, section outlined in green).

Pick up stitches more densely towards the neckline edge; the cabled motif has a tighter gauge than the Moss stitch section.

Row 2 (WS): Work Row 2 of Back Neck Chart, section outlined in green, SM, work Moss st to 1 st before end, P1.
Row 3 (RS): K1, work Moss st to M, work Row 3 of Back Neck Chart, section outlined in green.

Work through Row 7 of Back Neck Chart, section outlined in green. Continue Row 7 by casting on the remainder of the back neck sts. Do not work CO sts; rather, place the Right Back Shoulder sts back onto left hand needle, RS facing, and join the two sides by continuing across the RS of the Right Back sts in pattern per Row 7. 99 (103, 115, 117, 119, 127, 129) sts

Work Row 8.

Begin working the Main Back Chart for your size between M's. For sizes 32-36, work only one rep of the red bordered rep on the Main Back Chart Size 32, 36, 52, 56. For 52-56, work two reps. For 40, 44, 48, work two reps of the red bordered rep on the Main Back Chart Size 40, 44, 48. Work back in pattern, repeating 32-Row Main Chart, for 5.5 (5.5, 5.75, 4.5, 4.75, 5, 5.5)" from center of saddle strap at armhole edge, completing a WS Row. Note next RS Row for reference for front armhole shaping.

Armhole Shaping (Back)

Work all COs or increases to stay in Moss stitch pattern. Maintain the first and last sts as K1 on the RS. For M1, work M1r or M1p along right edge and M1l or M1p along left edge as you work.

All Sizes: Work both of the following rows 2 (6, 6, 8, 7, 7, 5) times:
(RS): K1, M1, work in pattern to 1 st before end, M1, K1.
(WS): Work in pattern.

Sizes 40, 44, 48, 52, 56 Only: Work both of the following rows – (–, 1, 2, 3, 3, 3) times:
(RS): CO 1 st and knit it, K1, M1, work in pattern to 1 st before end, M1, K1.
(WS): CO 1 st and purl it, work in pattern to end, incorporating sts into Moss st pattern.

Sizes 48, 52, 56 Only: Work both of the following rows – (–,–,–, 1, 2, 4) times:
(RS): CO 3 sts, work in pattern to end.
(WS): CO 3 sts (work as P1, then incorporate new sts and previous edge st into Moss st pattern), work in pattern to end, turn.

All Sizes (RS): CO 5 (5, 7, 7, 7, 9, 9) sts, PM for side, CO 5 (5, 7, 7, 7, 9, 9) sts. (Tip: CO 1 extra st at the end; when you join the pieces, work a K2tog with the last st of the current piece and the extra CO st.) Do not work CO sts or remainder of RS of row.

Break yarn. Place sts on scrap yarn and set back aside. 113 (125, 145, 155, 165, 183, 193) sts.

Right Front

With RS facing, PU and K 5 (5, 5, 6, 6, 7, 8) sts (Moss st section), PM, PU and K 20 sts (cable section) from edge of the right saddle strap. 25 (25, 25, 26, 26, 27, 28) sts.
Work Right Front Neckline chart, following as charted for neckline increases. See notes on chart regarding each size. 44 (45, 46, 48, 49, 50, 52) sts.
Work to RS row noted for back armhole shaping and begin armhole shaping as below. At the same time, complete the Right Front Neck Chart, then work even in established pattern, beginning with Row 1 of the Small Main Chart.

Armhole Shaping (Right Front)

Work all COs or increases to stay in Moss st pattern. Maintain the first and last sts as K1 on the RS. For M1, work M1r or M1p along right edge as you work.

All Sizes: Work both of the following rows 2 (6, 6, 8, 7, 7, 5) times:
(RS): K1, M1, work in pattern to end.
(WS): Work in pattern.

Sizes 40, 44, 48, 52, 56 Only: Work both of the following rows – (–, 1, 2, 3, 3, 3) times:
(RS): CO 1 st and knit it, incorporate next st into Moss stitch pattern, M1, work in pattern to end.
(WS): Work in pattern.

Sizes 48, 52, 56 Only: Work both of the following rows – (–,–,–, 1, 2, 4) times:
(RS): CO 3 sts (work as K1, then incorporate new sts and previous edge stitch into Moss stitch pattern), then work in pattern to end.
(WS): Work in pattern.

All Sizes: CO 5 (5, 7, 7, 7, 9, 9) sts, PM for side, CO 5 (5, 7, 7, 7, 9, 9) sts. (Tip: CO 1 extra st at the end; when you join the pieces, work a K2tog with the last st of the current piece and the extra CO st.) Do not work CO sts or remainder of RS of Row. Break yarn. Place sts on scrap yarn and set right front aside. 56 (61, 68, 74, 79, 87, 93) sts

Left Front

With RS facing, PU and K 20 sts (cable section), PM, PU and K 5 (5, 5, 6, 6, 7, 8) sts (Moss stitch section), from edge of the left saddle strap. 25 (25, 25, 26, 26, 27, 28) sts.

Work Left Front Neckline chart, following as charted for neckline increases. 44 (45, 46, 48, 49, 50, 52) sts.

Work to RS row noted for back armhole shaping and begin armhole shaping as below. At the same time, complete the Left Front Neck Chart, then work even in established pattern, beginning with Row 1 of the Small Main Chart. Remember to work the 2/1/2 RCP as a 2/1/2 LCP for the Left Front.

Armhole Shaping (Left Front)
Work all COs or increases to stay in Moss st pattern. Maintain the first st along the armhole as K1 on the RS. For M1, work M1l or M1p along left edge as you work.

All Sizes: Work both of the following rows 2 (6, 6, 8, 7, 7, 5) times:
(RS): Work in pattern to 1 st before end, M1, K1.
(WS): Work in pattern.

Sizes 40, 44, 48, 52, 56 Only: Work both of the following rows – (-, 1, 2, 3, 3, 3) times:
(RS): Work in pattern to 1 st before end, M1, K1.
(WS): CO 1 st and purl it, work in pattern to end.

Sizes 48, 52, 56 only: Work both of the following rows – (-,-,-, 1, 2, 4) times:
(RS): Work in pattern.
(WS): CO 3 sts (work as P1, then incorporate new sts and previous edge st into Moss stitch pattern), work in pattern to end, turn.
46 (51, 54, 60, 65, 69, 75) sts

Main Body

With RS of Left Front facing you, work in pattern to end of Small Main Chart (Left Side), work in Moss St to 6 sts before M (joining to back), K1, P2, K2, P1, SM, P1, K2, P2, K1, work in Moss St to Main Back Chart, work in pattern to end of Main Back Chart, work in Moss St to 6 sts before M (joining to Right Front), K1, P2, K2, P1, SM, P1, K2, P2, K1, work in Moss St to Small Main Chart (Right Side), work in pattern to end. 113 (125, 145, 155, 165, 183, 193) sts for back, 51 (56, 61, 67, 72, 78, 84) sts each front, 215 (237, 267, 289, 309, 339, 361) sts total. Work in pattern (maintaining Moss st and ribbing as established) for 2.25 (2.25, 2.5, 2.5, 3, 3, 3)".

Waist Shaping
Work all Increase or Decrease Rows on RS Row. Decreases incorporate the knit columns adjacent to the Moss stitch panel and the first Moss stitch. Work increases (shown as M1) as M1r or M1p to maintain Moss stitch pattern.

Dec Row (RS): Work in established pattern to 1 st before end of Small Main Chart (Left Side), SSK, work to 1 st before Back Chart, K2tog, work to 1 st before end of Back Chart, SSK, work to 1 st before Small Main Chart (Right Side), K2tog, work to end. 4 sts dec.

Work Dec Row once, then every 10th row two more times. 203 (225, 255, 277, 297, 327, 349) sts.

Work in pattern for 2" from the last decrease, ending with a WS row.

Inc Row (RS): Work in established pattern through end of Small Main Chart (Left Side), M1, work to Back Chart, M1, work through end of Back Chart, M1, work to Small Main Chart (Right Side), M1, work to end. 4 sts inc.
Work Inc Row once, then every 14th row two more times. 215 (237, 267, 289, 309, 339, 361) sts.

Work approximately 11.25 (11.25, 11.5, 11.5, 12, 12, 12)" from armhole, or 3" before desired start of ribbing, ending by working Row 14 or Row 30.

Ribbing
When working the section between side ribbing and chart (or chart and side ribbing) on setup for ribbing, increase (or) decrease sts in pattern (M1p or M1r, K2tog or P2tog) as needed to establish (K2, P2) ribbing.

Setup for Ribbing using Transition Row Charts (RS): *Work in pattern through appropriate transition chart, establish (K2, P2) ribbing (see note above) to side ribbing, work side ribbing, establish (K2, P2) ribbing (see note above) to chart, rep from *, work in pattern to end.

Work ribbing as established, complete chart, then work in ribbing as established for 3". BO in pattern.

Sleeves

Note for Small Main Chart: Continue working the repeat from where you left off. The sleeve will have ribbing to line up with the underarm ribbing of the sweater. Moss st panels flank the cable pattern. Order of work: Ribbing, Moss St, Cable pattern, Moss St, Ribbing. Remember to work the 2/1/2 RCP as a 2/1/2 LCP for the left sleeve.

Do not conceal wraps for the sleeves.

All decreases will be worked between the ribbing and Moss st sections: ribbing to last ribbing st, decrease with last ribbing and first Moss st, Moss st, cable, Moss st to last Moss st, decrease with Moss st and first ribbing, ribbing.

Starting from the underarm center and going in a clockwise direction, PU (do not knit, just pick up) 23 (24, 27, 30, 33, 36, 40) sts (PU 1 st in each CO st), place 35 sts from the saddle straps on needle, PU 23 (24, 27, 30, 33, 36, 40) sts. PM for beginning of rnd at underarm center. 81 (83, 89, 95, 101, 107, 115) sts.

Work short rows to shape sleeve cap as described below, but do NOT conceal wraps. I recommend setting up the Moss st pattern such that the st on either side of the chart is worked as a purl st; this will set up working the st after the W&T as K1.

Short Row 1 (RS): Join yarn beginning at st 24 (23, 26, 28, 30, 33, 37); work 0 (1, 1, 2, 3, 3, 3) sts in Moss st to saddle strap, work saddle strap in pattern, work 0 (1, 1, 2, 3, 3, 3) sts in Moss st, W&T next st. 35 (37, 37, 39, 41, 41, 41) sts worked, with 0 (1, 1, 2, 3, 3, 3) sts on either side of the Saddle Strap.

Short Row 2 (WS): Work in pattern to st where you joined the yarn, W&T next st.

Short Row 3: Work in pattern to wrapped st, W&T next st. Rep Short Row 3 until you have 7 (7, 9, 9, 9, 12, 12) sts unworked on the far side, ending with a WS Row (working its W&T).

Set Up Rnd 1 (partial rnd): Turn and begin working in the rnd to 6 sts before M, K1, P2, K2, P1.

Set Up Rnd 2 (full rnd): P1, K2, P2, K1, continue round in established pattern to end.

Work in the rnd in pattern until sleeve measures 1 (1.25, 1.5, 2, 2.25, 2.5, 2.5)" from underarm.

Dec Rnd: P1, K2, P2, SSK, K to 7 sts before end, K2tog, work in ribbing to end. 2 sts dec.
Repeat Dec Rnd every 13 (11, 10, 9, 9, 8, 7)th rnd another 6 (11, 12, 13, 4, 9, 12) times, then every 12 (-, -, -, 8, 7, 6)th rnd 4 (-, -, -, 10, 6, 5) times. 59 (59, 63, 67, 71, 75, 79) sts.

WE until sleeve measures approximately 18" from underarm or 2" less than desired length, completing Round 14 or 30 of the repeat.

Note: If you do reach your desired length and the round is in between Rounds 14 & 30, you can simply begin the ribbing for the Moss stitch portions of the sleeve, and work the motif in pattern until the nearest transition round. Conversely, if you are quite close to your desired length, and you've reached Round 14 or 30, start the ribbing transition for the cable pattern.

Cuff
Change to smaller needles.
Next Rnd: P1, (K2, P2) to motif (increasing or decreasing to establish in ribbing as needed), work appropriate Small Main Transition chart; K1, (P2, K2) to 1 st before end (increasing or decreasing as needed to establish ribbing), P1.
Work in established rib for 2". BO in pattern.

Collar and Buttonband
Length will vary on this cardigan depending on what repeat you ended on; thus, the directions for picking up sts along the front edge is based on picking up 6.33 sts/inch. For the collar, pick up at 5.5 sts/inch. Your final st count for each button band and the collar needs to be a multiple of 4 sts. Plan ahead! Note: For my sample, size medium, I picked up 120 sts per side for the buttonbands, and 156 sts for the collar, trying to keep the K2 columns flowing out of the cables as best possible.

Right Front
With smaller needles, beginning at the lower corner of the right front, RS facing, PU and K 6.33 sts/inch along the front edge to the point where the neckline shaping ended (last knitted CO row). Remember to pick up a multiple of 4 sts.
Next Row (WS): P3, (K2, P2) to 1 st before end, P1.
Next Row (RS): K3, (P2, K2) to 1 st before end, K1.
Rep until buttonband measures 2". BO in pattern.

Left Front
With smaller needles, beginning at the upper corner of the left front where the neckline shaping ended (last knitted CO row), RS facing, PU and K 6.33 sts/inch along the front edge. Remember to pick up a multiple of 4 sts.
Next Row (WS): P3, (K2, P2) to 1 st before end, P1.
Next Row (RS): K3, (P2, K2) to 1 st before end, K1.
Continue in pattern until buttonband measures 0.75", ending on a WS Row.

Decide where you would like your buttonholes and how many you'd like to work. I worked 6 buttonholes, with 5 knit ribs between each buttonhole. Buttonholes are worked as a SSK of the last knit st of the last counted knit rib and the first purl st, a double YO, then K2tog, then work in pattern to next buttonhole placement. This nestles the buttonholes in the P2 sections of the rib.

Work buttonholes along right front as follows:
RS: Work in pattern to first buttonhole placement, ending with the first knit st on the knit rib before desired buttonhole placement, *SSK, double YO, K2tog, work in pattern to next buttonhole placement; repeat from * for each buttonhole, work in pattern to end.
WS: Work in pattern, working the double YOs as P1 TBL twice.
RS: Work in established ribbing.
Continue in established ribbing until buttonband measures 2". BO in pattern.

Collar
With smaller needles, beginning at the upper corner of the right front buttonband, RS facing, PU and K approximately 5.5 sts/inch along the collar to the end of the left front buttonband shaping ended (last knitted CO row). Remember to pick up a multiple of 4 sts.
Next Row (WS): K3, (P2, K2) to 1 st before end, K1.
Next Row (RS): P3, (K2, P2) to 1 st before end, P1.
Rep until collar measures 4" tall. BO in pattern.

Finishing
Weave in ends, wash and block. I recommend blocking to slightly larger than the schematic measurements, as once unpinned, the cables will cause the sweater to pull in. Sew on buttons.

Legend:

- ☐ **knit**
  RS: knit stitch
  WS: purl stitch
- • **purl**
  RS: purl stitch
  WS: knit stitch
- ■ **no stitch**
- **P2TOG**
  purl 2 stitches together
- **P2**
  purl 2
- **P1, M1P**
  RS: p1, make one purl
  WS: k1, make one right
- **pick up and knit**
- **knitted cast on**
- **wrap and turn**
- **cast on**
- **bind off**
- **pattern repeat**
- **right back shoulder**
- **left back shoulder**
- **2/1 RCP K2TOG**
  Sl 1 st to RH needle; Sl next st to CN and hold in back; Sl st from RH needle to LH needle; K2TOG, K1, P1 from CN.
- **2/1 LCP SSK**
  Sl 2 sts to CN and hold in front, P1, Sl sts back to LH needle, K1, SSK.
- **2/1 LCP**
  Sl 2 sts to CN and hold in front; P1; K2 from CN.
- **2/1 RCP**
  Sl 1 st to CN and hold in back; K2; P1 from CN.
- **2/2 LC**
  Sl 2 STS to CN and hold in front; K2; K2 from CN.
- **2/2 RC**
  Sl 2 STS to CN and hold in back; K2; K2 from CN.
- **2/2 LCP2TOG**
  Sl P st to RH needle, Sl 2 sts to CN and hold in front; Sl P st back to LH needle, P2TOG, P1; K2 from CN.
- **2/2 RCP2TOG**
  Sl 2 STS to CN and hold in back; K2; P1 from CN, Sl last P st to LH needle, P2TOG.
- **2/2 RCP**
  Sl 2 STS to CN and hold in back; K2; P2 from CN.
- **2/2 LCP**
  Sl 2 STS to CN and hold in front; P2; K2 from CN.
- **2/2 RCKP**
  Sl 2 STS to CN and hold in back; K2; P1, K1 from CN.
- **2/2 LCPK**
  Sl 2 STS to CN and hold in front; P1, K1; K2 from CN.
- **2/2 RCPK**
  Sl 2 STS to CN and hold in back; K2; P1, K1 from CN.
- **2/2 LCKP**
  Sl 2 STS to CN and hold in front; K1, P1; K2 from CN.
- **2/1/2 RPC**
  Sl 2 STS to 1st CN and hold in back; Sl 1 ST to 2nd CN and hold in back; K2; P1 from 2nd CN; K2 from 1st CN.
- **2/1/2 LPC**
  Sl 2 STS to 1st CN and hold in front; Sl 1 ST to 2nd CN and hold in back; K2; P1 from 2nd CN; K2 from 1st CN.
- Work a 2/1/2 LCP when working the left saddle strap, sleeve, and front

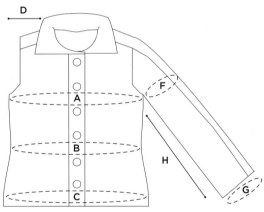

A 32 (36, 40, 44, 48, 52, 56)"
B 30 (34, 38, 42, 46, 50, 54)"
C 32 (36, 40, 44, 48, 52, 56)"
D 3 (3.25, 3.5, 3.5, 3.75, 3.75, 4)"
F 12.5 (13, 14, 15, 16, 17.25, 18.75)"
G 7.25 (7.5, 7.75, 8.25, 8.5, 9, 9.25)"
H 20"
I 6.25 (6.75, 7.25, 7.75, 8.25, 8.5, 8.75)"
J 14.25 (14.25, 14.5, 14.5, 15, 15, 15)"
K 20.25 (20.5, 21.25, 21.75, 22.75, 23.25, 23.75)"

Back Neck 32 36

Back Neck 40 44 48

Back Neck 52 56

Back Transition Row 15 32 36 52 56

Back Transition Row 15 40 44 48

Back Transition Row 31 32 36 52 56

Back Transition Row 31 40 44 48

66 Sionann Cardi

Main Back Chart 32 36 52 56

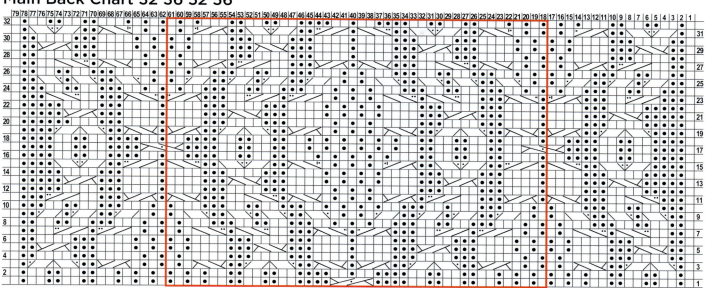

Main Back Chart 40 44 48

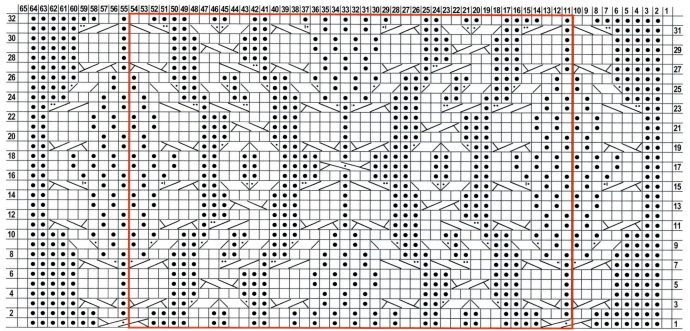

Right Front Neckline

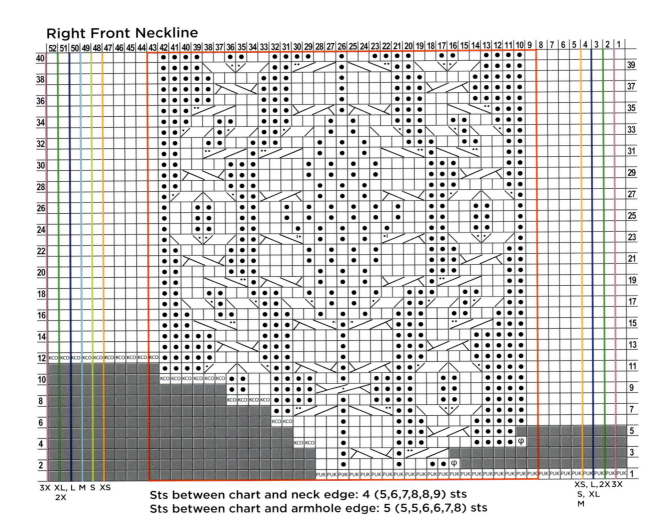

Sts between chart and neck edge: 4 (5,6,7,8,8,9) sts
Sts between chart and armhole edge: 5 (5,5,6,6,7,8) sts

Right Saddle Tab, Front, Sleeve Transition Row 14

Sionann Cardi 69

Swatch Chart

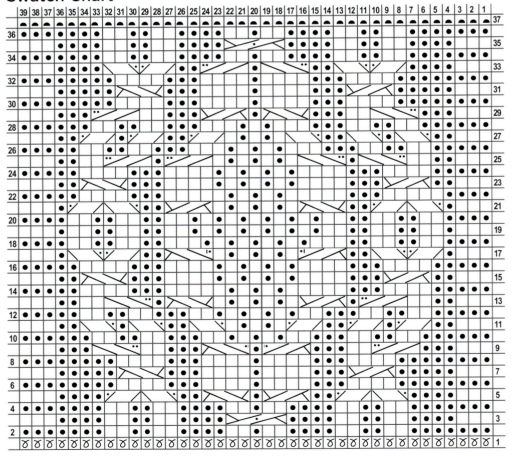

Sionann Cardi

Right Saddle, Front, Sleeve Transition Row 30

Sionann Cardi

Small Main Chart Transition Row 14

Small Main Chart

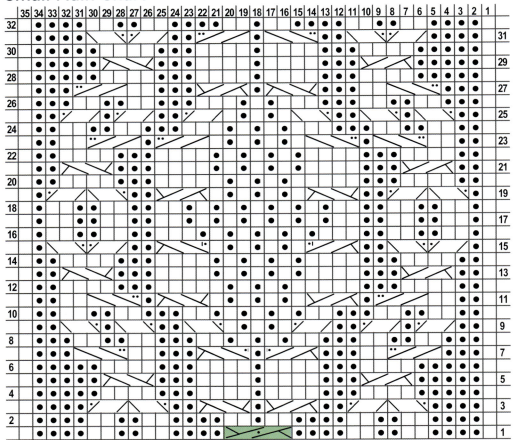

Small Main Chart Transition Row 30

SNOHOMISH PULLOVER

by Allison Griffith

FINISHED MEASUREMENTS
36.5 (42.5, 45, 48.5, 52, 55.5, 58, 64, 67.5)" finished bust measurement; garment is meant to be worn with 2-4" of positive ease

YARN
Knit Picks Wool of the Andes Worsted (100% Peruvian Highland Wool; 110 yards/50g): Grizzly Heather 25641, 10 (11, 12, 12, 13, 13, 14, 15, 16) balls

NEEDLES
US 7 (4.5mm) circular needles and DPNs or a second circular for two circulars technique, or size to obtain gauge
US 6 (4mm) circular needles and DPNs or a second circular for two circulars technique, or one size smaller than size to obtain gauge

NOTIONS
Yarn Needle, Stitch Markers, Stitch Holders or Scrap Yarn, Cable Needle

GAUGE
18 sts and 28 rows = 4" in Chart A in the rnd on larger needles, blocked
22 sts = 4" in 1x1 Rib in the rnd on smaller needles, blocked
1 repeat of Chart B = 1.5" wide on larger needles, blocked
1 repeat of Chart C = 1.2" wide on larger needles, blocked

Snohomish Pullover

Notes:
This sweater is worked in the round from the bottom up. The body is worked first, and sleeves are worked separately. The body and sleeves are joined at the underarms, and the yoke is worked. The neck is worked flat, then the collar is picked up and knit.

For the majority of this pattern, charts are worked in the round, read from the bottom up, from right to left. When indicated, work charts flat (read from the bottom up, right to left on odd-numbered rows, and left to right on even-numbered rows).

Be aware that the cable patterns used in this sweater stretch significantly when blocked. Taking the time to make an accurate gauge swatch will be very helpful in properly sizing your sweater.

1x1 Rib (worked in the round over an even number of sts)
All Rounds: (K1, P1) to end of rnd.

Increase
Use any invisible increase that you prefer. M1 (http://tutorials.knitpicks.com/make-1-increase/) or Knit into the Stitch Below (http://tutorials.knitpicks.com/knit-into-stitch-below/) increases both work well for this pattern.

Backwards Loop CO
Follow the instructions available here: http://tutorials.knitpicks.com/loop-cast-on/

DIRECTIONS

Body
With smaller circular needle, CO 180 (208, 222, 238, 252, 266, 280, 310, 324) sts. PM for beginning of rnd, being careful not to twist sts.
Work in 1x1 Rib for 2 (2, 2, 2, 2, 2.5, 2.5, 2.5, 2.5)".
Switch to larger circular needle and K 1 rnd, increasing 20 (24, 26, 26, 28, 30, 32, 34, 36) sts, spaced evenly around body. 200 (232, 248, 264, 280, 296, 312, 344, 360) sts.

Cable Set-up Row: Work *Chart A 4 (5, 5, 6, 7, 8, 8, 9, 10) times, P1, K1, P1, Chart B once, P1, K1, P1, Chart C 5 (6, 7, 7, 7, 7, 8, 9, 9) times, P1, K1, P1, Chart B once, P1, K1, P1, Chart A 4 (5, 5, 6, 7, 8, 8, 9, 10) times; rep from * once more. If desired, place additional markers to make following the established pattern simpler.

Work in established pattern until sweater measures 14 (14, 14, 15, 15, 15, 16, 16, 16)" from CO edge (or desired length), ending with Chart C Row 8.

Work 7 (8, 9, 9, 10, 11, 12, 12, 13) sts of next row in established pattern. Transfer all sts to scrap yarn and set aside.

Sleeves (make 2)
With smaller DPNs, CO 44 (44, 52, 52, 60, 68, 68, 76, 76) sts. PM for beginning of rnd (center of underarm), being careful not to twist sts.
Work in 1x1 Rib for 2 (2, 2, 2, 2, 2.5, 2.5, 2.5, 2.5)".
Switch to larger DPNs and K 1 rnd, increasing 8 sts, evenly spaced around sleeve. 52 (52, 60, 60, 68, 76, 76, 84, 84) sts.

Sleeve Set-up Row: Work Chart A 2 (2, 2, 2, 3, 3, 3, 4, 4) times, P1, K1, P1, Chart B once, P1, K1, P1, Chart C 1 (1, 2, 2, 2, 3, 3, 3, 3) time(s), P1, K1, P1, Chart B once, P1, K1, P1, Chart A 2 (2, 2, 2, 3, 3, 3, 4, 4) times. If desired, place additional markers to make following the established pattern simpler.

Sleeve Shaping
Work in established cable pattern while simultaneously working shaping as follows. As you increase, work increased sts as part of additional repeats of Chart A.

Work even for 11 (7, 7, 5, 5, 4, 4, 4, 3) rnds, following established cable pattern.
Increase Round: Work 1 st, inc 1, work to 1 st before end, inc 1, work 1. 2 sts inc.
Continue in established pattern, working an Increase Round every 11 (7, 7, 6, 6, 5, 5, 5, 4)th round until you have worked 8 (12, 12, 16, 16, 20, 20, 20, 24) increase rounds. 68 (76, 84, 92, 100, 116, 116, 124, 132) sts.

Continue in established pattern with no more shaping until your sleeve measures 17 (17, 17, 18, 18, 18, 19, 19, 19)" from CO edge (or desired length), ending with Chart C Row 8.

First Sleeve (Right Sleeve): Work 7 (8, 9, 9, 10, 11, 12, 12, 13) sts of next row in established pattern. Break yarn, leaving an 18" tail. Transfer sts to scrap yarn, keeping underarm marker in place. Set aside.

Second Sleeve (Left Sleeve): Work 7 (8, 9, 9, 10, 11, 12, 12, 13) sts of next row in established pattern, keeping underarm marker in place. Do not break yarn. Continue directly to next section.

Join Sleeves and Body
Continue to work charts as established, while at the same time joining sleeves and body.
With the larger circular needle, work across Left Sleeve to 7 (8, 9, 9, 10, 11, 12, 12, 13) sts before underarm marker, PM, transfer 14 (16, 18, 18, 20, 22, 24, 24, 26) sleeve sts to scrap yarn or stitch holder, removing underarm marker; work 86 (100, 106, 114, 120, 126, 132, 148, 154) Front Body sts, PM, transfer 14 (16, 18, 18, 20, 22, 24, 24, 26) body sts to scrap yarn or stitch holder; work across Right Sleeve to 7 (8, 9, 9, 10, 11, 12, 12, 13) sts before underarm marker, PM, transfer 14 (16, 18, 18, 20, 22, 24, 24, 26) sleeve sts to scrap yarn or stitch holder, removing underarm marker; work 86 (100, 106, 114, 120, 126, 132, 148, 154) Back Body sts, PM (end of rnd). Transfer 14 (16, 18, 18, 20, 22, 24, 24, 26) body sts to scrap yarn or stitch holder. 280 (320, 344, 376, 400, 440, 448, 496, 520) sts.

Work 7 (5, 3, 3, 3, 3, 3, 1, 1) rnds without shaping, continuing charts as established.

Yoke

Work Yoke decreases as follows, while continuing charts as established. Note: Cables should meet and mirror each other at raglan increases. As sts are decreased, some cables will "disappear" into the yoke shaping.

Round 1: (SSK, work to 2 sts before the next M, K2tog, SM) four times. 8 sts dec.
Round 2: (K1, work to 1 st before next marker, K1, SM) four times.

Rep Rnds 1 and 2 following established pattern as possible, a total of 17 (21, 23, 24, 25, 26, 28, 31, 33) times, until 144 (152, 160, 184, 200, 232, 224, 248, 256) sts remain, ending with Round 2. 20 (18, 20, 26, 30, 42, 36, 38, 40) sts each Sleeve, 52 (58, 60, 66, 70, 74, 76, 86, 88) sts each for Front and Back. Decreases will now continue simultaneously with Neck shaping.

Neck

Set up for neck shaping as follows: Break yarn. SL Left Shoulder sts to RH needle without working, SM, SL the next 14 (15, 15, 16, 17, 18, 16, 20, 19) sts to RH needle.

Join yarn and BO 24, (28, 30, 34, 36, 38, 44, 46, 50) sts in pattern. Work as established to end of row (front left edge of neck), continuing to work decreases as established before and after each st marker. From now on, work back and forth. Turn work, ready to begin a WS row.

Continue working cables and shoulder shaping as established (decreasing before and after each st marker on RS rows), while **at the same time** working the following Neck Shaping. Omit step if 0. Note: Remove markers as necessary when sts are bound off.

Neck Shaping
BO 4 sts at the beginning of the next 0 (0, 2, 2, 2, 2, 2, 4, 4) rows.
BO 3 sts at the beginning of the next 4 rows.
BO 2 sts at the beginning of the next 4 (4, 2, 2, 2, 2, 2, 0, 0) rows.

BO remaining sts.

Collar

With smaller DPNs, PU 58 (68, 74, 80, 86, 94, 98, 108, 114) sts around neck of sweater. Work in the rnd in 1x1 Rib for .75". BO very loosely in pattern.

Finishing

Use the Kitchener Stitch to close up armpits. Weave in ends, and block firmly to measurements, being careful not to stretch ribbing.

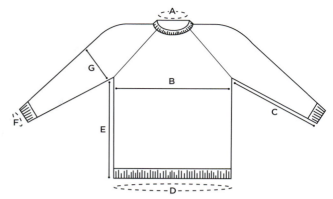

A 10.5 (12.25, 13.5, 14.5, 15.75, 17, 17.75, 19.5, 20.75)"
B 37.5 (43.5, 46, 49.5, 53, 56.5, 59, 65, 68.5)"
C 17 (17, 17, 18, 18, 19, 19, 19)"
D 32.75 (37.75, 40.25, 43.25, 45.75, 48.25, 51, 56.25, 59)"
E 14 (14, 14, 15, 15, 15, 16, 16, 16)
F 8 (8, 9.5, 9.5, 11, 12.25, 12.25, 13.75, 13.75)"
G 14 (15.75, 17, 18.75, 20.5, 23.5, 23.5, 25.25, 27)"

Chart A

4	3	2	1	
		●	●	4
		●	●	3
●	●			2
●	●			1

Chart B

8	7	6	5	4	3	2	1	
								8
								7
╲╱╲╱╲╱╲╱								6
								5
								4
								3
								2
								1

Chart C

8	7	6	5	4	3	2	1	
●	●					●	●	8
●	●					●	●	7
	·	╲	╲	╱	╱	·		6
		●	●	●	●			5
		●	●	●	●			4
		●	●	●	●			3
	╲	╲	·	·	╱	╱		2
●	●					●	●	1

Legend:

□ **knit**
RS: knit stitch
WS: purl stitch

● **purl**
RS: purl stitch
WS: knit stitch

C2 over 2 right
SL2 to CN, hold in back, K2, K2 from CN

C2 over 2 left
SL2 to CN, hold in front, K2, K2 from CN

C2 over 2 right P
SL2 to CN, hold in back, K2, P2 from CN

C2 over 2 left P
SL2 to CN, hold in front, P2, K2, from CN

TORQUE PONCHO

by Nadya Stallings

FINISHED MEASUREMENTS
37 (41.5, 45.25)" wide x 27.75 (28.5, 29.25)" long; garment is meant to be worn with 1-5" of positive ease

YARN
Knit Picks Swish Worsted (100% Superwash Merino Wool; 110 yards/50g): Delft Heather 24095, 17 (19, 21) balls

NEEDLES
US 5 (3.75mm) 24" or longer circular needles, or size to obtain gauge

NOTIONS
Yarn Needle, Stitch Markers, Cable Needles Scrap Yarn or Stitch Holders

GAUGE
19.5 sts and 23.5 rows = 4" over Cable stitch patterns and St st combined, blocked

For pattern support, contact nadyastallings@gmail.com

Torque Poncho

Notes:
The Torque Poncho is a simple construction of two rectangular panels, with the novel addition of a standard collar. Each of them is worked flat from the bottom up. The neckline is shaped with short rows at front, and after seaming the shoulders is finished with the collar, which is also shaped with short rows.
Work chart RS rows (odd numbers) from right to left, and WS rows (odd numbers) from left to right.

Garter Stitch (worked flat)
All Rows: K.

Stockinette Stitch (St st, worked flat)
Row 1 (RS): K.
Row 2 (WS): P.
Rep Rows 1-2 for pattern.

Wrap and Turn (W&T): Sl next st WYIF, return yarn to back. PM on left needle and return the Sl st to the left needle, turn.

DIRECTIONS
Back
The Back panel is worked flat from bottom up. If necessary, use stitch markers to divide certain stitch sections for easier following of the stitch patterns.
CO 182 (204, 222) sts.
Work 7 rows in Garter st ending with a WS row.

Row 1 (RS): K4, P1, work Row 1 of Chart 1, P1, K7 (18, 27), work Row 1 of Chart 2 over the next 106 sts with 3 total pattern repeats, K7 (18, 27), P1, work Row 1 of Chart 1 again, P1, K4.
Row 2 (WS): K5, work Row 2 of Chart 1, K1, P7 (18, 27), work Row 2 of Chart 2 with 3 total pattern repeats, P7 (18, 27), K1, work Row 2 of Chart 1 again, K5.
WE as established for 160 (164, 168) more rows, repeating Rows 3-6 of Chart 1 and Rows 3-22 of Chart 2, or until back panel reaches 27.75 (28.5, 29.25)" from CO.

BO 72 (81, 88) shoulder sts, K 38 (42, 46) neck sts, BO remaining 72 (81, 88) shoulder sts.
Transfer remaining 38 (42, 46) live neck sts to scrap yarn or stitch holder.

Front
Work as for Back until 7 (row wise) repeats of Chart 2 Rows 3-22 are completed. Cont in pattern for 6 (10, 14) more rows, ending with a WS row. PM in the center of the Front.

Neckline Shaping
Next Row (RS): Work in pattern to beginning of Chart 2 section, switch to Chart 3 for your size and work 14 rows from Chart 3, working the rest of Left Front as established. Work Row 15 from Chart 3 and then P to M, working wrapped sts together with wraps, SM. From this point of the row work Chart 4 for your size, working the rest of Right Front as established.

Next Row (WS): P to end of the row working wrapped sts together with wraps.
BO 72 (81, 88) shoulder sts in beginning of the next 2 rows; K all sts beside BO sts. Transfer remaining 38 (42, 46) neck sts onto scrap yarn.

Finishing
Block Back and Front to measurements. Sew shoulders. With a few sts, tack together each side at the underarms, approximately 11 (11.75, 12.25)" down from the shoulder seam, creating an armhole opening.

Collar
Beginning at front neckline center and with RS facing, K across held 76 (84, 92) live neck sts of Front and Back. Work flat in Garter st for 7 rows, ending with a WS row.

Collar Shaping
Short Row 1 (RS): K38 (42, 46) sts, W&T.
Short Row 2 and all WS rows through Row 12: K to end of the row.
Short Row 3: K32 (35, 39) sts, W&T.
Short Row 5: K26 (28, 32) sts, W&T.
Short Row 7: K20 (21, 24) sts, W&T.
Short Row 9: K14 (14, 16) sts, W&T.
Short Row 11: K7 (7, 8) sts, W&T.
Short Row 13: K to end of the row working wrapped sts together with wraps.
Short Row 14 (WS): K38 (42, 46) sts, W&T.
Short Row 15 and all RS rows through Row 25: K to end of the row.
Short Row 16: K32 (35, 39) sts, W&T.
Short Row 18: K26 (28, 32) sts, W&T.
Short Row 20: K20 (21, 24) sts, W&T.
Short Row 22: K14 (14, 16) sts, W&T.
Short Row 24: K7 (7, 8) sts, W&T.
Short Row 26: K to end of the row, working wrapped sts together with wraps
Work two more rows in Garter st.
Loosely BO.

Finishing
Weave in remaining ends. Block Collar if desired.

Chart 1

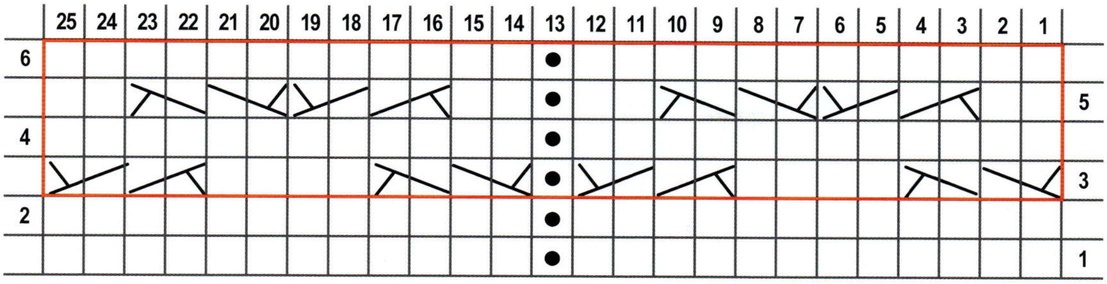

Chart 2

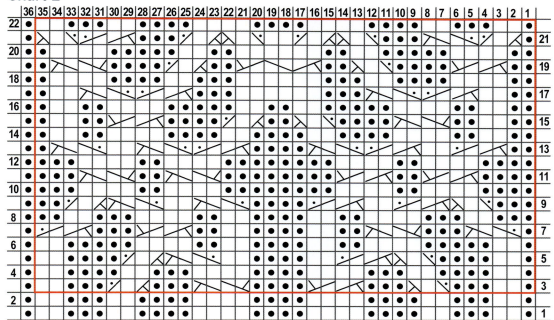

Legend:

- ☐ **knit** — RS: knit stitch / WS: purl stitch
- ⊡ **purl** — RS: purl stitch / WS: knit stitch
- ■ **no stitch**
- ☐ **pattern repeat**
- ⓦ **wrap and turn**
- **c2 over 1 right P** — SL1 to CN, hold in back. K2, p1 from CN
- **c2 over 1 left P** — SL2 to CN, hold in front. P1, K2 from CN
- **c2 over 2 right** — SL2 to CN, hold in back. K2, K2 from CN
- **c2 over 2 left** — SL2 to CN, hold in front. K2, K2 from CN
- **c2 over 2 left P** — SL2 to CN, hold in front. P2, K2 from CN
- **c2 over 2 right P** — SL2 to CN, hold in back. K2, P2 from CN
- **c2 over 2 right/2 left** — SL2 to 1st CN at back; SL2 to 2nd CN at front; K2 from LN; K2 from 2nd CN; K2 from 1st CN

Torque Poncho   85

Chart 3-37

Chart 3-41.5

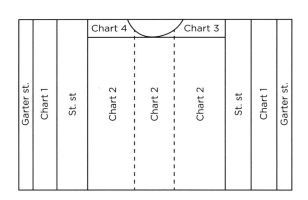

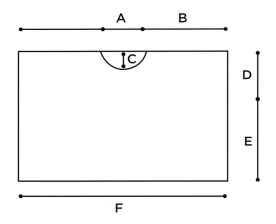

A 7.5 (8.25, 9)"
B 14.75 (16.5, 18)"
C 2.75"
D 11 (11.75, 12.5)"
E 16.75"
F 37 (41.5, 45.25)"

Chart 3-45.25

Torque Poncho

Chart 4-37

Chart 4-41.5

Chart 4-45.25

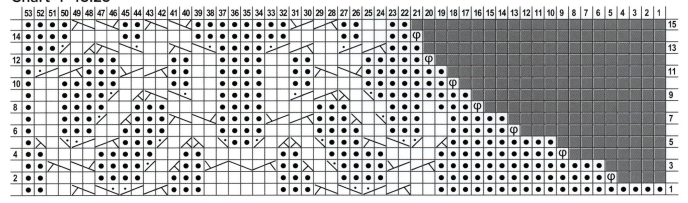

Torque Poncho

ARISAIG

by Luise O'Neill

FINISHED MEASUREMENTS
Triangular shape; 45" short edge, 68" straight edge, 82" curved edge

YARN
Knit Picks Wool of the Andes Sport (100% Peruvian Highland Wool; 137 yards/50g): Claret Heather 25303, 12 balls

NEEDLES
US 4 (3.5mm) 32" or longer circular needle, or size to obtain gauge

NOTIONS
Yarn Needle, Stitch Marker, Cable Needle, Size E-4 (3.5mm) Crochet Hook for Provisional Cast On

GAUGE
Chart A 87-st Cable Panel = 10.5" wide, blocked
21 sts and 32 rows = 4" over Chart B, blocked

For pattern support, contact patternsupport@impeccableknits.ca

Arisaig

Notes:
Arisaig, located on the Sunrise Trail along the Northumberland Strait that separates Nova Scotia and Prince Edward Island, is a small Nova Scotia village founded in the late 1700s by Scottish immigrants who named it after their home on the west coast of Scotland. A seaside marvel, the Arisaig Sea Cliffs are world-famous for their fossils. So, wrap yourself in comfort as you share in the natural beauty of its breath-taking seascape.

Arisaig is a triangle shawl knit from the shortest side to the tip. The shawl begins with a Double Chain Cast On which mimics an I-Cord cast on but avoids the long loops that the latter often creates. A crochet hook is used for this cast on. The cable panel is worked along the right edge (as knit) of the shawl. The edges are worked in slipped-stitch mock I-cord for a lovely rounded finish. The pattern is fully charted. Read RS chart rows (odd numbers) from right to left, and WS rows (even numbers) from left to right.

Make 2 Purl (M2P): Insert tip of LH needle, from front to back, to lift yarn between needles, P into front and back of lifted loop. 2 sts inc.

Double Chain Cast On
A picture tutorial for the Double Chain Cast On can be found at the designer's website: https://impeccableknits.wordpress.com/2016/08/13/double-chain-cast-on/
Step 1: Make a slip knot and place it on the LH needle. This is only to anchor the yarn, it is not counted as a st and will be removed later.
Step 2: Place crochet hook behind needle to the right of the slip knot.
Step 3: Take yarn behind crochet hook, bring yarn up and over the needle then around the needle to the back and over the front of the crochet hook.
Step 4: Catching yarn, pull crochet hook through to front (between the slip knot and the new loop formed on needle.
Step 5: Bring crochet hook to back of needle by swinging the tip of the hook to the left and under the needle. Do not catch the yarn during this maneuver.
Step 6: Take yarn behind crochet hook, bring it up and over the needle then around the needle to the back and over the front of the crochet hook.
Step 7: Catching yarn, pull crochet hook through to front and through loop on crochet hook.
Rep Steps 5-7 until all sts are CO. Sl loop from crochet hook onto LH needle. Remove initial slip knot.

DIRECTIONS

Bottom Border
Using the Double Chain Cast On, CO 252 sts.

Row 1 (RS): K1, Sl1 WYIF, K to last 2 sts, Sl1 WYIF, K1.
Row 2 (WS): Sl1 WYIF, K1, Sl1 WYIF, K to last 3 sts, Sl1 WYIF, K1, Sl1 WYIF.

Rows 3-4: Rep Rows 1 - 2.
Row 5: K1, Sl1 WYIF, K67, PM, K to last 2 sts, Sl1 WYIF, K1.
Row 6 (Inc Row): Sl1 WYIF, K1, Sl1 WYIF, K to M, SM, K1, P2, K1, M2P, P2, K1, P2, M1, K1, P2, K1, M1, (P2, K1) twice, P2, (M1, K1) twice, P2, K3, M2P, P4, M2P, K3, P2, M1, K1, M1, (K1, P) 3 times, M1, K1, P2, M1, *(K1, P2) twice, M2P; rep from * once more, K1, P2, K1, Sl1 WYIF, K1, Sl1 WYIF. 270 sts.

Main Pattern
Row 1 (RS): Work Row 1 of Chart A, SM, work Row 1 of Chart B. 269 sts.
Row 2 (WS): Work Row 2 of Chart B to M, SM, work Row 2 of Chart A.
Rep these two rows, working subsequent rows of each chart, until 95 sts remain (87 sts before the M and 8 sts after) having completed a Row 26 of Chart A and Row 6 of Chart B. 95 sts.

Work Chart C. 59 sts.

Work Chart D. 3 sts.
Turn. P3tog.

Cut yarn leaving 6" tail; pull tail through remaining loop.

Finishing
Weave in ends, wash and block to diagram.

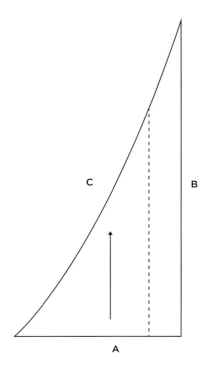

A 45"
B 68"
C 82"

Arisaig Chart A

Legend:

- ☐ **knit**
  RS: knit stitch
  WS: purl stitch
- • **purl**
  RS: purl stitch
  WS: knit stitch
- ■ **no stitch**
- ⧄ **K2TOG**
  knit 2 together
- ▭ **pattern repeat**
- **slip**
  RS: Slip stitch as if to purl, holding yarn in back
  WS: Slip stitch as if to purl, holding yarn in front
- **slip wyif**
  RS: Slip stitch as if to purl, with yarn in front
  WS: Slip stitch as if to purl, with yarn in back

- **Right Twist**
  Skip the first stitch, knit into 2nd stitch, then knit skipped stitch. Slip both stitches from needle together OR K2TOG leaving sts on LH needle, then K first ST again, SL both STS off needle.
- **Left Twist**
  SL1 to CN, hold in front. K1, K1 from CN
- **Right Twist, purl bg**
  SL1 to CN, hold in back. K1, P1 from CN
- **Left Twist, purl bg**
  SL1 to CN, hold in front. P1, K1 from CN
- **c2 over 1 left P**
  SL2 to CN, hold in front. P1, K2 from CN
- **c2 over 1 right P**
  SL1 to CN, hold in back. K2, P1 from CN
- **c2 over 1 right**
  SL1 to CN, hold in back. K2, K1 from CN
- **c2 over 1 left**
  SL2 to CN, hold in front. K1, K2 from CN
- **c1 over 2 left**
  SL1 to CN, hold in front. K2, K1 from CN
- **c1 over 2 right**
  SL2 to CN, hold in front. K2, K1 from CN
- **c2 over 2 right**
  SL2 to CN, hold in back. K2, K2 from CN
- **c2 over 2 left**
  SL2 to CN, hold in front. K2, K2 from CN

Arisaig

Arisaig Chart B

Arisaig Chart C

Arisaig Chart D

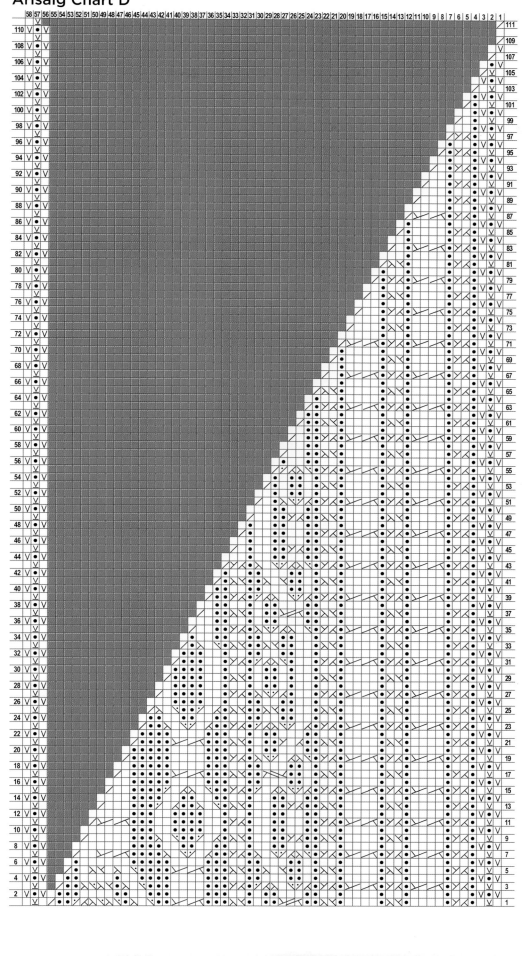

DUN LAOGHAIRE

by Triona Murphy

FINISHED MEASUREMENTS
31.75 (35.75, 39.25, 44.25, 47.75, 52.25, 55.75, 59.75)" finished bust measurement; garment is meant to be worn with 2" of positive ease

YARN
Knit Picks Wool of the Andes Worsted (100% Peruvian Highland Wool; 110 yards/50g): Shire Heather 25988, 9 (10, 11, 13, 15, 17, 18, 20) balls

NEEDLES
US 7 (4.5mm) DPNs, 24 (24, 24, 24, 32, 32, 32, 32)" circular needle, 40" or longer circular needle for BO, or size to obtain gauge

NOTIONS
Yarn Needle, Stitch Markers, Cable Needle, Scrap Yarn or Stitch Holder

GAUGE
21 sts and 28 rows = 4" in St st, blocked
11.5 (11.5, 13.75, 13.75, 15.5, 15.5, 19.25, 19.25)" = width of Cable Panel (including first and last P sts), blocked

For pattern support, contact triona@trionadesigns.com

Dun Laoghaire

Notes:

This cabled pullover, named for the charming Irish seaside town of Dun Laoghaire, features updated details like 3/4 sleeves, dolman shaping, and a boat neck.

The sweater is worked flat from the bottom up in two identical front and back pieces. Sleeve sts are increased gradually near the underarm and then the rest are cast on all at once to work simultaneously with the upper part of the sweater. Short rows shape the shoulders and then the upper sleeve edges and shoulders are joined using the Three-Needle Bind Off method. Sides and lower sleeve edges are seamed together using Mattress stitch.

The cable panel on the front and back is slightly different in larger sizes to maintain proportions. Work as directed for each size.

When working neckline shaping, maintain cable patterns as much as possible. If there aren't enough sts to work a cable cross, work these sts in St st or Reverse St st as appropriate to where you are in the pattern. The charts are read from right to left on RS rows (even numbers) and left to right on WS rows (odd numbers).

1x1 Rib (worked flat over an even number of sts)
Row 1 (RS): (K1, P1) to end.
Row 2 (WS): (K1, P1) to end.
Rep Rows 1-2 for pattern.

1x1 Rib (worked in the rnd over an even number of sts)
All Rnds: (K1, P1) to end.

Small Cable (worked flat over 4 sts)
Row 1 (WS): P4.
Row 2 (RS): C2 over 2 left.
Row 3: P4.
Row 4: K4.
Rep Rows 1-4 for pattern.

Medium Cable (worked flat over 15 sts)
Row 1 (WS): K5, P2, K1, P2, K5.
Row 2 (RS): P5, c2 over 2 left/purl bg, P5.
Row 3: K5, P2, K1, P2, K5.
Row 4: P4, c2 over 1 right P, P1, c2 over 1 left P, P4.
Row 5: K4, P2, K3, P2, K4.
Row 6: P3, c2 over 1 right P, K1, P1, K1, c2 over 1 left P, P3.
Row 7: K3, P2, (K1, P1) twice, K1, P2, K3.
Row 8: P2, c2 over 1 right P, (K1, P1) twice, K1, c2 over 1 left P, P2.
Row 9: K2, P2, (K1, P1) three times, K1, P2, K2.
Row 10: P1, c2 over 1 right P, (K1, P1) three times, K1, c2 over 1 left P, P1.
Row 11: K1, P2, (K1, P1) four times, K1, P2, K1.
Row 12: C2 over 1 right P, (K1, P1) four times, K1, c2 over 1 left P.
Row 13: P2, (K1, P1) five times, K1, P2.
Row 14: K2, P3, K2, P1, K2, P3, K2.
Rep Rows 1-14 for pattern.

Large Cable (worked flat over 24 sts)
Row 1 (WS): K2, P6, K8, P6, K2.
Row 2 (RS): P2, c3 over 3 left, P8, c3 over 3 left, P2.
Row 3: K2, P6, K8, P6, K2.
Row 4: P2, K6, P8, K6, P2.
Row 5: K2, P6, K8, P6, K2.
Row 6: P2, K6, P8, K6, P2.
Row 7: K2, P6, K8, P6, K2.
Row 8: P2, c3 over 3 left, P8, c3 over 3 left, P2.
Row 9: K2, P6, K8, P6, K2.
Row 10: P1, c3 over 1 right P, c3 over 1 left P, P6, c3 over 1 right P, c3 over 1 left P, P1.
Row 11: K1, P3, K2, P3, K6, P3, K2, P3, K1.
Row 12: C3 over 1 right P, P2, c3 over 1 left P, P4, c3 over 1 right P, P2, c3 over 1 left P.
Row 13: (P3, K4) three times, P3.
Row 14: K3, P4, c3 over 1 left P, P2, c3 over 1 right P, P4, K3.
Row 15: P3, K5, P3, K2, P3, K5, P3.
Row 16: C3 over 1 left P, P4, c3 over 1 left P, c3 over 1 right P, P4, c3 over 1 right P.
Row 17: K1, P3, K5, P6, K5, P3, K1.
Row 18: P1, c3 over 1 left P, P4, c3 over 3 right, P4, c3 over 1 right, P1.
Row 19: K2, P3, K4, P6, K4, P3, K2.
Row 20: P2, c3 over 1 left P, P2, c3 over 1 right P, c3 over 1 left P, P2, c3 over 1 right P, P2.
Row 21: K3, P3, (K2, P3) three times, K3.
Row 22: P3, c3 over 1 left P, c3 over 1 right P, P2, c3 over 1 left P, c3 over 1 right P, P3.
Row 23: K4, (P6, K4) twice.
Row 24: (P4, c3 over 3 left) twice, P4.
Row 25: K4, P6, K4, P6, K4.
Row 26: P3, c3 over 1 right P, c3 over 1 left P, P2, c3 over 1 right P, c3 over 1 left P, P3.
Row 27: K3, P3, K2, P3, K2, P3, K2, P3, K3.
Row 28: P2, (c3 over 1 right P, P2, c3 over 1 left P) twice, P2.
Row 29: K2, P3, K4, P6, K4, P3, K2.
Row 30: P1, c3 over 1 right P, P4, c3 over 3 right, P4, c3 over 1 left P, P1.
Row 31: K1, P3, K5, P6, K5, P3, K1.
Row 32: C3 over 1 right P, P4, c3 over 1 right P, c3 over 1 left P, P4, c3 over 1 left P.
Row 33: P3, K5, P3, K2, P3, K5, P3.
Row 34: K3, P4, c3 over 1 right P, P4, c3 over 1 left P, P4, K3.
Row 35: (P3, K4) three times, P3.
Row 36: C3 over 1 left P, P2, c3 over 1 right P, P4, c3 over 1 left P, P2, c3 over 1 right P.
Row 37: K1, P3, K2, P3, K6, P3, K2, P3, K1.
Row 38: P1, c3 over 1 left P, c3 over 1 right P, P6, c3 over 1 left P, c3 over 1 right P, P1.
Rep Rows 1-38 for pattern.

C2 over 2 left: Sl2 to CN, hold in front. K2, K2 from CN.

C2 over 2 left/purl bg: Sl3 to CN, hold in front. K2, Sl center st from CN back to left hand needle and purl it. K2 from CN.

C2 over 1 right P: Sl1 to CN, hold in back. K2, P1 from CN.

C2 over 1 left P: Sl2 to CN, hold in front. P1, K2 from CN.

C3 over 3 left: Sl3 to CN, hold in front. K3, K3 from CN.

C3 over 3 right: Sl3 to CN, hold in back. K3, K3 from CN.

C3 over 1 right P: Sl1 to CN, hold in back. K3, P1 from CN.

C3 over 1 left P: Sl3 to CN, hold in front. P1, K3 from CN.

Make 1 Left (M1L): PU the bar between st just worked and next st and place on LH needle as a regular stitch; knit through the back loop (left-slanting increase).

Make 1 Right (M1R): PU the bar between st just worked and next st and place on LH needle backwards (incorrect st mount), then knit through the front loop (right-slanting increase).

DIRECTIONS
Front
With circular needle, CO 100 (110, 120, 132, 144, 156, 166, 176) sts. Do not join. Working back and forth in rows, work 1x1 Rib for 1", ending with a RS row.

Work the following Set-up Row for your size only as below.
Set-up Row Sizes 31.75, 35.75, 39.25, 44.25 (WS): P13 (18, 17, 23 —, —, —, —), K2 (2, 4, 4, —, —, —, —), PM, work Row 1 of Medium Cable over next 15 sts, PM, K2 (2, 4, 4, —, —, —, —), work Row 1 of Small Cable over next 4 sts, K2 (2, 4, 4, —, —, —, —), PM, work Row 1 of Large Cable over next 24 sts, PM, K2 (2, 4, 4, —, —, —, —), work Row 1 of Small Cable over next 4 sts, K2 (2, 4, 4, —, —, —, —), PM, work Row 1 of Medium Cable over next 15 sts, PM, K2 (2, 4, 4, —, —, —, —), P13 (18, 17, 23, —, —, —, —).

Set-up Row Sizes 47.75, 52.25, 55.75, 59.75 (WS): P— (—, —, —, 23, 29, 24, 29), PM, K— (—, —, —, 2, 2, 4, 4), work Row 1 of Small Cable over next 4 sts, K— (—, —, —, 2, 2, 4, 4), PM, work Row 1 of Medium Cable over next 15 sts, PM, K— (—, —, —, 2, 2, 4, 4), work Row 1 of Small Cable over next 4 sts, K— (—, —, —, 2, 2, 4, 4), work Row 1 of Small Cable over next 4 sts, K— (—, —, —, 2, 2, 4, 4), PM, work Row 1 of Large Cable over next 24 sts, PM, K— (—, —, —, 2, 2, 4, 4) work Row 1 of Small Cable over next 4 sts, K— (—, —, —, 2, 2, 4, 4), work Row 1 of Small Cable over next 4 sts, K— (—, —, —, 2, 2, 4, 4), PM, work Row 1 of Medium Cable over next 15 sts, PM, K— (—, —, —, 2, 2, 4, 4), work Row 1 of Small Cable over next 4 sts, K— (—, —, —, 2, 2, 4, 4), PM, P— (—, —, —, 23, 29, 24, 29).

Work next row for your size only as below.
Next Row Sizes 31.75, 35.75, 39.25, 44.25 (RS): K13 (18, 17, 23 —, —, —, —), P2 (2, 4, 4, —, —, —, —), SM, work Row 2 of Medium Cable over next 15 sts, SM, P2 (2, 4, 4, —, —, —, —), work Row 2 of Small Cable over next 4 sts, P2 (2, 4, 4, —, —, —, —), SM, work Row 2 of Large Cable over next 24 sts, SM, P2 (2, 4, 4, —, —, —, —), work Row 2 of Small Cable over next 4 sts, P2 (2, 4, 4, —, —, —, —), SM, work Row 2 of Medium Cable over next 15 sts, SM, P2 (2, 4, 4, —, —, —, —), K13 (18, 27, 23, —, —, —, —).

Next Row Sizes 47.75, 52.25, 55.75, 59.75 (RS): K— (—, —, —, 23, 29, 24, 29), SM, P— (—, —, —, 2, 2, 4, 4), work Row 2 of Small Cable over next 4 sts, P— (—, —, —, 2, 2, 4, 4), SM, work Row 2 of Medium Cable over next 15 sts, SM, P— (—, —, —, 2, 2, 4, 4), work Row 2 of Small Cable over next 4 sts, P— (—, —, —, 2, 2, 4, 4), work Row 2 of Small Cable over next 4 sts, P— (—, —, —, 2, 2, 4, 4), SM, work Row 2 of Large Cable over next 24 sts, SM, P— (—, —, —, 2, 2, 4, 4), work Row 2 of Small Cable over next 4 sts, P— (—, —, —, 2, 2, 4, 4), work Row 2 of Small Cable over next 4 sts, P— (—, —, —, 2, 2, 4, 4), SM, work Row 2 of Medium Cable over next 15 sts, SM, P— (—, —, —, 2, 2, 4, 4), work Row 2 of Small Cable over next 4 sts, P— (—, —, —, 2, 2, 4, 4), SM, K— (—, —, —, 23, 29, 24, 29).

Continue in pattern, working the next row of each cable pattern and Reverse St st between markers as established, until work measures 4" from CO edge, ending with a WS row.

Waist Shaping
Waist Decrease Row (RS): K2, K2tog, work in pattern to last 4 sts, SSK, K2. 2 sts dec.
Work Waist Decrease Row every 6th row, three more times. 92 (102, 112, 124, 136, 148, 158, 168) sts.
Work even in pattern as set for 2", ending with a WS row.
Waist Increase Row (RS): K2, M1L, work in pattern to last 2 sts, M1R, K2. 2 sts inc.
Work Waist Increase Row every 6th (6th, 6th, 6th, 4th, 4th, 4th, 4th) row, three more times. 100 (110, 120, 132, 144, 156, 166, 176) sts.
Work even in pattern as set until piece measures 13.25 (13.25, 12.5, 12.5, 12.5, 11.75, 11.75, 11)" from CO edge, ending with a WS row.

Sleeve Shaping
Sleeve Increase Row (RS): K1, M1R, work in pattern to last st, M1L, K1. 2 sts inc.
Work Sleeve Increase Row every 4th row, two more times. 106 (116, 126, 138, 150, 162, 172, 182) sts.
Then work Sleeve Increase Row every 2nd row, 5 (5, 8, 8, 8, 10, 10, 13) times. 116 (126, 142, 154, 166, 182, 192, 208) sts.
Work one WS row even.
Next Row (RS): CO 48 sts at the beginning of the row using the Cable Cast On method, knit these new sts, work to end of the row in pattern as set.
Next Row (WS): CO 48 sts at the beginning of the row using the Cable Cast On method, purl these new sts, work in pattern to other set of new sts, purl to end. 212 (222, 238, 250, 262, 278, 288, 304) sts.
Continue in pattern, working new sleeve sts in St st, until sleeve height measures 2.75 (3.25, 3.75, 4.25, 5, 5.5, 5.75, 6)" from new CO sts, ending with a WS row.

Neck Shaping
Next Row (RS): Work 93 (98, 105, 111, 116, 124, 129, 137) sts in pattern, slip these sts to a holder or scrap yarn for Left Front and Sleeve, BO center 26 (26, 28, 28, 30, 30, 30, 30) sts, work in pattern to end.
You will now be working back and forth on the 93 (98, 105, 111, 116, 124, 129, 137) sts for the Right Front and Sleeve only.

Right Front and Sleeve

Work one WS row even in pattern, then BO sts at the beginning of the next five RS rows as follows:

RS Row 1: BO 6 sts.
RS Row 2: BO 4 (4, 4, 4, 4, 4, 5, 5) sts.
RS Row 3: BO 3 (3, 4, 4, 4, 4, 4, 4) sts.
RS Row 4: BO 3 sts.
RS Row 5: BO 1 st.

When all BOs are completed, 76 (81, 87, 93, 98, 106, 110, 118) sts remain for Right Front and Sleeve. Work these sts even in pattern until sleeve height measures 5.5 (6, 6.5, 7, 7.75, 8.25, 8.75, 9.25)" from new CO sts, ending with a WS row.

Shape Shoulder

Short Row 1 (RS): Work in pattern for 23 (23, 27, 27, 27, 31, 31, 31) sts, W&T.
Next Row (WS): Work in pattern to end, turn.
Short Row 2 (RS): Work in pattern to 6 (6, 7, 7, 7, 8, 8, 8) sts before last wrapped st, W&T.
Next Row (WS): Work in pattern to end, turn.
Rep last 2 rows twice more. 4 sts wrapped.
Next Row (RS): Work to end of row in pattern, picking up wraps as you come to them.
Cut yarn. Slip all sts to a holder or scrap yarn.

Left Front and Sleeve

Slip 93 (98, 105, 111, 116, 124, 129, 137) sts from holder or scrap yarn back to needles. Rejoin yarn to neck edge with the WS facing, then BO sts at the beginning of the next five WS rows as follows:

WS Row 1: BO 6 sts.
WS Row 2: BO 4 (4, 4, 4, 4, 4, 5, 5) sts.
WS Row 3: BO 3 (3, 4, 4, 4, 4, 4, 4) sts.
WS Row 4: BO 3 sts.
WS Row 5: BO 1 st.

When all BOs are completed, 76 (81, 87, 93, 98, 106, 110, 118) sts remain for Left Front and Sleeve. Work these sts even in pattern until sleeve height measures 5.5 (6, 6.5, 7, 7.75, 8.25, 8.75, 9.25)" from new CO sts, ending with a RS row.

Shape Shoulder

Short Row 1 (WS): Work in pattern for 23 (23, 27, 27, 27, 31, 31, 31) sts, W&T.
Next Row (RS): Work in pattern to end, turn.
Short Row 2 (WS): Work in pattern to 6 (6, 7, 7, 7, 8, 8, 8) sts before last wrapped st, W&T.
Next Row (RS): Work in pattern to end, turn.
Rep last 2 rows twice more. 4 sts wrapped.
Next Row (WS): Work to end of row in pattern, picking up wraps as you come to them.
Cut yarn. Slip all sts to a holder or scrap yarn.

Back

Work as for Front.

Finishing

Wash and block front and back pieces to diagram.

Slip the Right Front and Sleeve sts onto one end of longer circular needle and the Right Back and Sleeve sts onto the other end. Holding the RS of the fabric together with WS facing out, use a DPN to work a Three-Needle Bind Off at the top of the sleeve. Repeat with Left Front and Sleeve and Left Back and Sleeve.

Using Mattress stitch, sew bottom of sleeves and sides together.

Neckband

Using circular needle and beginning at top left shoulder seam, PU and K 148 (148, 168, 168, 172, 172, 188, 188) sts around entire neckline, approximately 3 sts in every 4 rows and 1 st in each BO st. The exact number doesn't matter, just make sure your final number is a multiple of 2. Join for working in the rnd and PM.
Work 1x1 Rib for 1".
BO all sts in pattern.

Cuff

Using DPNs and beginning at bottom sleeve seam, PU and K 46 (50, 56, 60, 64, 70, 74, 76) sts around armhole, approximately 2 sts in every 3 rows. The exact number doesn't matter, just make sure your final number is a multiple of 2. Join for working in the rnd and PM.
Work 1x1 Rib for 1".
BO all sts in pattern.
Rep for other armhole.

Weave in ends, wash and block again if desired.

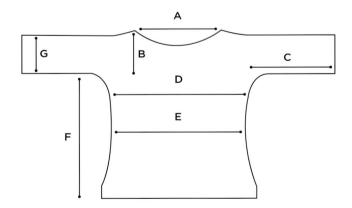

A 11.5 (11.5, 12.25, 12.25, 12.5, 12.5, 13, 13)"
B 6.75 (7.25, 7.75, 8.25, 9, 9.5, 10, 10.5)"
C 10.75 (10.75, 11.25, 11.25, 11.25, 11.5, 11.5, 12.25)"
D 16.25 (18.25, 20, 22.5, 24.25, 26.5, 28.25, 30.25)"
E 14.75 (16.75, 18.5, 21, 22,75, 25, 26.75, 28.75)"
F 16"
G 5.5 (6, 6.5, 7, 7.25, 8.25, 8.75, 9.25)"

Note: Measurements are of flat garment pieces, before sewing together or adding ribbed bands.

Small Cable Chart

	4	3	2	1	
					4
3					
					2
1					

Medium Cable Chart

Legend:

- ☐ **knit**
  RS: knit stitch
  WS: purl stitch

- • **purl**
  RS: purl stitch
  WS: knit stitch

- **c2 over 1 right P**
  SL1 to CN, hold in back. K2, P1 from CN

- **c2 over 1 left P**
  SL2 to CN, hold in front. P1, K2 from CN

- **c2 over 2 left**
  SL2 to CN, hold in front. K2, K2 from CN

- **cross 2 over 2 left/purl bg**
  SL3 to CN, hold in front. K2, SL center ST from CN back to left hand needle and purl it. K2 from CN

- **c3 over 1 right P**
  SL1 to CN, hold in back. K3, P1 from CN

- **c3 over 1 left P**
  SL3 to CN, hold in front. P1, then K3 from CN

- **c3 over 3 right**
  SL3 to CN, hold in back. K3, K3 from CN

- **c3 over 3 left**
  SL3 to CN, hold in front. K3, K3 from CN

Dun Laoghaire 103

Large Cable Chart

GREN STOLE

by Courtney Spainhower

FINISHED MEASUREMENTS
20" at widest point x 60.5" long

YARN
Knit Picks Andean Treasure (100% Baby Alpaca; 110 yards/50g): Embers Heather 23486, 11 balls

NEEDLES
US 4 (3.5mm) straight or circular needles, or size to obtain gauge

NOTIONS
Yarn Needle, Stitch Markers, Cable Needle

GAUGE
27 sts and 34 rows = 4" over Inc Chart or Dec Chart, blocked
29 sts and 34 rows = 4" over sts 12-40 of Large Cable Chart, blocked and measured on WS

For pattern support, contact cspainhower@gmail.com

Gren Stole

Notes:
The stole is worked lengthwise with tapered ends, and fully charted. For Inc Chart 2 and Dec Chart 1, repeat pattern twice between red bars to marked center stitches, work as charted between markers, then repeat pattern twice between red bars, and work to end of row. When working the charts read RS rows (odd numbers) from right to left, and WS rows (even numbers) from left to right.

2/2 RC: Sl 2 sts to CN, hold in back; K2, K2 from CN.
2/2 LC: Sl 2 sts to CN, hold in front; K2, K2 from CN.
3/3 RC: Sl 3 sts to CN, hold in back; K3, K3 from CN.
3/3 LC: Sl 3 sts to CN, hold in front; K3, K3 from CN.
1/2 RPC: Sl 2 sts to CN, hold in back; K1, P2 from CN.
1/2 LPC: Sl 1 st to CN, hold in front; P2, K1 from CN.

DIRECTIONS
Increase End
Loosely CO 23 sts.
Work Inc Chart 1. 75 sts.
Work Inc Chart 2, removing markers on Row 107. 131 sts.
Next Row (WS): (K1, P1) 2 times, K1, P4, K1, P1, K1, PM, (K17, KFB) 5 times, K to last 12 sts, PM, K1, P1, K1, P4, K1, (P1, K1) 2 times. 136 sts.

Body
Markers will not line up with the Row 7 pattern repeat, you may wish to shift them for this row.
Work Rows 1-36 of Large Cable chart 8 times, then rep Rows 1-13 once more.

Decrease End
Next Row (WS): (K1, P1) 2 times, K1, P4, K1, P1, K1, (K16, K2tog) 5 times, K to last 12 sts, K1, P1, K1, P4, K1, (P1, K1) 2 times. 131 sts.
Work Dec Chart 1 placing markers for center 19 sts as follows: Work Row 1 over first 56 sts, PM, work over next 19 sts, PM, work to end. Continue through Row 52. 79 sts.
Work Dec Chart 2. 23 sts.
BO loosely in pattern.

Finishing
Weave in ends, wash and block to measurements.

Increase Chart 1

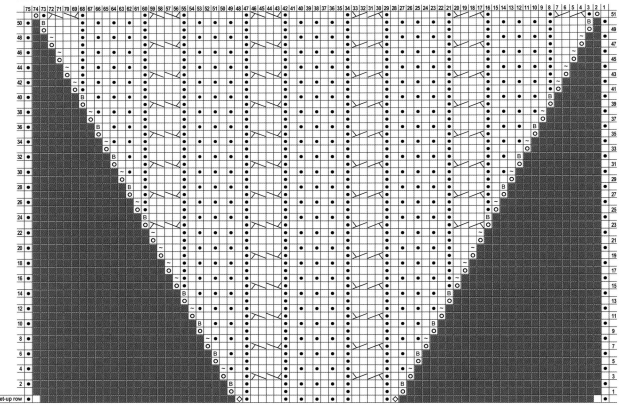

Increase Chart 2

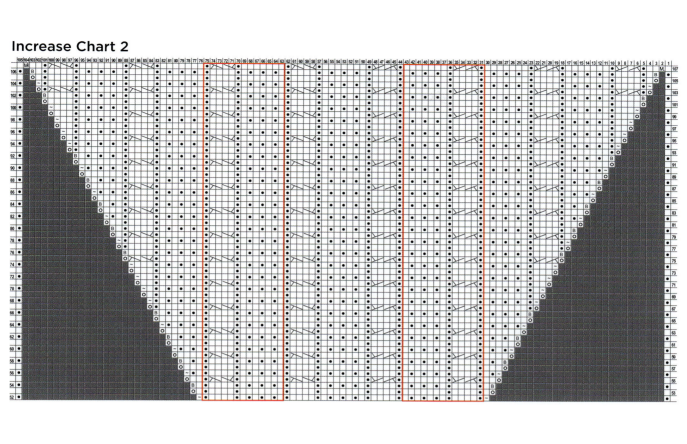

Legend:

	knit RS: knit stitch WS: purl stitch
▣	purl RS: purl stitch WS: knit stitch
■	no stitch
O	YO Yarn Over
B	knit TBL Knit stitch through back loop
~	purl TBL Purl stitch through the back loop
M	make one left Place a firm backward loop over the right needle, so that the yarn end goes towards the front
MR	make one right Place a firm backward loop over the right needle, so that the yarn end goes towards the back
◨	SSK SL, SL, K these 2 STS together
◪	K2TOG knit two STS together
◨	P2TOG purl 2 STS together
◪	P2TOG TBL purl 2 STS together through the back loop
▭	pattern repeat
◇	place marker
	c1 over 2 right P SL2 to CN, hold in back. K1, P2 from CN
	c1 over 2 left P SL1 to CN, hold in front. P2, K1 from CN
	c2 over 2 right SL2 to CN, hold in back. K2, K2 from CN
	c2 over 2 left SL2 to CN, hold in front. K2, K2 from CN
	c3 over 3 right SL3 to CN, hold in back. K3, then K3 from CN
	c3 over 3 left SL3 to CN, hold in front. K3, K3 from CN

Gren Stole 109

Large Cable Chart

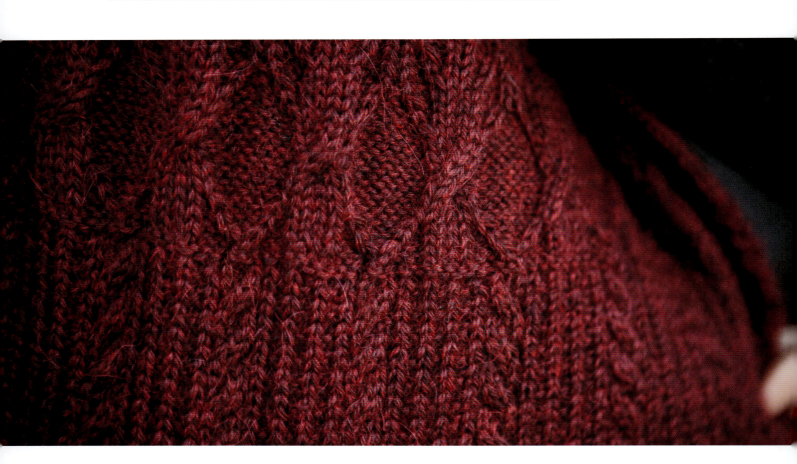

Decrease Chart 2

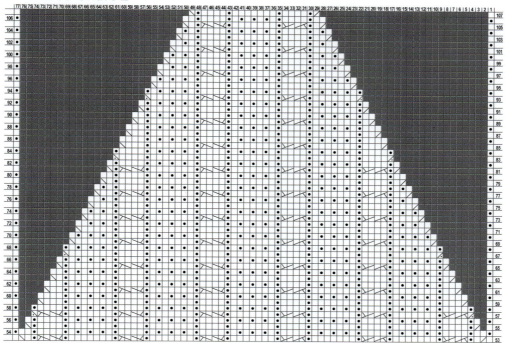

Decrease Chart 1

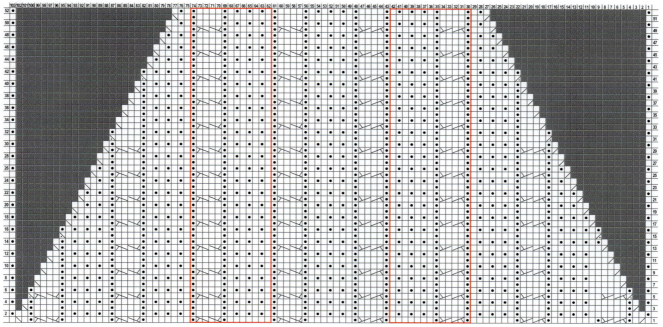

Gren Stole 111

STUDIO CARDIGAN

by Nadya Stallings

FINISHED MEASUREMENTS
40.25 (42.75, 47.75, 50.75, 55.25, 58.75, 63.25, 69.75)" finished bust measurement; garment is meant to be worn with 5-6" of positive ease

YARN
Knit Picks Wool of the Andes Sport (100% Peruvian Highland Wool; 137 yards/50g): Dove Heather 25656, 15 (16, 18, 20, 21, 22, 24, 26) balls

NEEDLES
US 4 (3.5mm) 24" or longer circular needles, DPN's, spare straight needles for 3-Needle BO and pocket, or size to obtain gauge

NOTIONS
Yarn Needle, Stitch Markers, Cable Needle, Scrap Yarn or Stitch Holder

GAUGE
26 sts and 27.25 rows = 4" over Gauge Chart, blocked
20 sts and 40 rows = 4" in Garter st, blocked

For pattern support, contact nadyastallings@gmail.com

Studio Cardigan

Notes:
Cardigan is worked flat as one piece from the hem to the armholes, and then in pieces. A moderate width shawl collar along with front borders is worked as you go. Insert pockets are located at the sides.

There are two different cable patterns included in this design, as well as Garter stitch and Rev St st sections. For this reason, instructions suggest using plenty of stitch markers in the beginning of work, to separate the pattern sections.

Garter Stitch (worked flat)
Row 1: K.
Rep Row 1 for pattern.

Reverse Stockinette Stitch (Rev St st, worked flat)
Row 1 (RS): P.
Row 2 (WS): K.
Rep Rows 1-2 for pattern.

Garter Stitch (worked in the rnd)
Rnd 1: K
Rnd 2: P
Rep Rnds 1-2 for pattern.

Reverse Stockinette Stitch (Rev St st, worked in the rnd)
Rnd 1: P.
Rep Rnd 1 for pattern.

Wrap and Turn (W&T): Sl next st WYIF, return yarn to back. PM on left needle and return the slipped st to the left needle, turn. Note: use another pair of M's for W&T, use different M's than for sleeve center sts. Keep center st M's at their place for stitch pattern reference.

3-Needle Bind Off, a tutorial can be found at: http://tutorials.knitpicks.com/3-needle-bind-off/
Hold the WS of the knitting tog with the needle points facing to the right. Insert the third needle into the first st on each of the needles K-wise, starting with the front needle. Work a knit st, pulling the loop through both of the sts you have inserted the third needle through. Sl the first st off of each of the needles. Repeat this motion. Each time you complete a second st, pass the first finished st over the second and off of the needle.

DIRECTIONS
Body
The body is worked flat from the bottom up. Side decreases and pocket inserts occur simultaneously, read through entire body instructions before proceeding.
CO 220 (236, 256, 268, 292, 308, 328, 360) sts.
Hem, Rows 1-5: Work in Garter st ending with WS row.

Inc Row (RS): K9, PM, K3 (3, 5, 4, 4, 4, 4, 6), (M1, K2) 5 (5, 6, 8, 8, 10, 10, 11) times, K0 (0, 2, 4, 4, 4, 4, 6), (K2, M1) 5 (5, 6, 8, 8, 10, 10, 11) times, K3 (3, 5, 4, 4, 4, 4, 6), PM, K12 (16, 12, 5, 12, 6, 13, 12), PM, K3, (M1, K2) 5 times, (K2, M1) 5 times, K3, PM, K6 (10, 6, 11, 6, 12, 7, 6), PM, K3 (3, 2, 2, 5, 5, 4, 4), (M1, K2) 3 (3, 5, 5, 6, 6, 8, 10) times, K0 (0, 2, 2, 2, 2, 4, 4), (K2, M1) 3 (3, 5, 5, 6, 6, 8, 10) times, K3 (3, 2, 2, 5, 5, 4, 4), PM, K3, (M1, K2) 5 times, (K2, M1) 5 times, K3, PM, K3 (3, 2, 2, 5, 5, 4, 4), (M1, K2) 3 (3, 5, 5, 6, 6, 8, 10) times, K0 (0, 2, 2, 2, 2, 4, 4), (K2, M1) 3 (3, 5, 5, 6, 6, 8, 10) times, K3 (3, 2, 2, 5, 5, 4, 4), PM, K6 (10, 6, 11, 6, 12, 7, 6), PM, K3, (M1, K2) 5 times, (K2, M1) 5 times, K3, PM, K12 (16, 12, 5, 12, 6, 13, 12), PM, K3 (3, 5, 4, 4, 4, 4, 6), (M1, K2) 5 (5, 6, 8, 8, 10, 10, 11) times, K0 (0, 2, 4, 4, 4, 4, 6), (K2, M1) 5 (5, 6, 8, 8, 10, 10, 11) times, K3 (3, 5, 4, 4, 4, 4, 6), PM, K9. 282 (298, 330, 350, 378, 402, 430, 474) sts.
Next Row (WS): K.
Row 1 (RS): K8, P1, SM, work from Chart 1 to next M, SM, P to next M, SM, work from Chart 2 to next M, SM, P to next M, SM, work from Chart 1 to next M, SM, work from Chart 2 to next M, SM, work from Chart 1 to next M, SM, P to next M, SM, work from Chart 2 to next M, SM, P to next M, SM, work from Chart 1 to next M, SM, P1, K8.
Row 2: K9, SM, work from Chart 1 to next M, SM, K to next M, SM, work from Chart 2 to next M, SM, K to next M, SM, work from Chart 1 to next M, SM, work from Chart 2 to next M, SM, work from Chart 1 to next M, SM, K to next M, SM, work from Chart 2 to next M, SM, K to next M, SM, work from Chart 1 to next M, SM, K9.
Cont in pattern for 32 more rows ending with WS row.

Dec Row (RS): Work in pattern to 2 sts before third M, P2tog, SM, cont in pattern to next M, SM, P2tog, cont in pattern to 2 sts before ninth M, P2tog, SM, cont in pattern to next M, SM, P2tog, cont in pattern to end of the row. 4 sts dec.
Rep Dec Row every 34th row 4 more times ending with WS row. 262 (278, 310, 330, 358, 382, 410, 454) sts.
Transfer 70 (74, 82, 87, 94, 100, 107, 118) Front sts on each side onto scrap yarn. 122 (130, 146, 156, 170, 182, 196, 218) Back sts.

Pockets
AT THE SAME TIME work as instructed above for 86 rows of Chart 2 ending with Row 12 (WS) of Chart.
Transfer pocket sts (first and last sets of Chart 2 sts) onto scrap yarn, leaving all other sts on working needle.
With WS facing and straight needles, PU but do not knit 36 sts within pocket markers, 38 rows below held sts, taking care to pick up the sts from the same row for both pockets. Beginning with next row (RS) and joining another yarn ball, work in St st (K on RS, P on WS) for 38 rows or until the pocket back panel reaches the live sts on the working needle. Break yarn and transfer pocket panel sts onto the working needle. Cont in pattern, as instructed above.

Block Body
Weave in ends. Block Body to measurements.

Pocket Trim
Facing Pocket RS transfer 36 live Pocket sts on straight needle from right to left.
Row 1 (WS): (K2tog, K2) 4 times, K2tog twice, (K2, SSK) 4 times. 26 sts.
Cont in Garter stitch for 5 rows, ending with RS row, BO.
Repeat with another Pocket.

Sew Pocket inserts to the Body on WS. Sew Pocket trims on RS.

Back

Armhole Shaping

Row 1 (RS): P to first M, remove M, cont in pattern to last M, remove M, P to last 6 (6, 6, 7, 7, 7, 8, 8) sts, place these sts onto scrap yarn.

Row 2 (WS): K to M, SM, work in pattern to last 6 (6, 6, 7, 7, 7, 8, 8) sts, place these sts on scrap yarn. 110 (118, 134, 142, 156, 168, 180, 202) sts.

Cont in pattern for 46 (50, 52, 56, 56, 60, 62, 62) more rows, or until armhole depth reaches 7 (7.5, 8, 8.5, 8.5, 9, 9.5, 9.5)". BO 32 (33, 40, 43, 49, 54, 59, 68) shoulder sts at the beginning of the next 2 rows.

Place 46 (52, 54, 56, 58, 60, 62, 66) neck sts onto scrap yarn.

Front Left

Armhole shaping and Shawl Collar Shaping 1

Facing WS, transfer 45 (45, 57, 68, 68, 81, 81, 93) sts onto working needle, PM, transfer next 19 (23, 19, 12, 19, 12, 18, 17) sts onto working needle. Place remaining 6 (6, 6, 7, 7, 7, 8, 8) underarm sts on scrap yarn. 64 (68, 76, 80, 87, 93, 99, 110) sts. Beginning next row (RS), work in Rev St st to the M, then work from Chart 3 for your size to end of the row.
WE until Chart 3 is completed.

Next Row (RS): K.

Next Row (WS): K 32 (35, 36, 37, 38, 39, 40, 42) collar sts, BO 32 (33, 40, 43, 49, 54, 59, 68) shoulder sts.

Collar Shaping 2

Work in Garter st for 24 (28, 30, 30, 30, 32, 34, 34) rows.

Short Row 1 (RS): K

Short Row 2 (WS): K to last 7 (7, 8, 8, 8, 8, 8, 9) sts, W&T.

Short Row 3: K 7 (7, 8, 8, 8, 8, 8, 9) sts, PM, K to end of the row.

Short Row 4 and all WS Short Rows: K to M, SM, W&T.

Short Row 5: K 6 (7, 7, 7, 8, 8, 8, 8) sts, PM, K to end of the row.

Short Row 7: K 6 (7, 7, 7, 7, 8, 8, 8) sts, PM, K to end of the row.

Short Row 9: K all sts working wrapped sts tog with wraps.

Short Row 10: K

Transfer all collar sts onto scrap yarn

Front Right

Armhole shaping and Shawl Collar shaping 1

Facing WS, place 6 (6, 6, 7, 7, 7, 8, 8) underarm sts on scrap yarn. Transfer next 19 (23, 19, 12, 19, 12, 18, 17) sts onto working needle, PM, transfer remaining 45 (45, 57, 68, 68, 81, 81, 93) Right Front sts onto working needle. 64 (68, 76, 80, 87, 93, 99, 110) sts.

Beginning next row (RS) work from Chart 4 for your size to the M, then work in Rev St st to end of the Row.
WE until Chart 4 is completed.

Next Row (RS): K.

Next Row (WS): BO 32 (33, 40, 43, 49, 54, 59, 68) shoulder sts, K to end of the row. 32 (35, 36, 37, 38, 39, 40, 42) collar sts.

Collar Shaping 2

Work in Garter st for 24 (28, 30, 30, 30, 32, 34, 34) rows.

Short Row 1 (RS): K to last 7 (7, 8, 8, 8, 8, 8, 9) sts, W&T.

Short Row 2: K 7 (7, 7, 8, 8, 8, 8, 9) sts, PM, K to end of the row.

Short Row 3 and all RS Short Rows: K to M, SM, W&T.

Short Row 4: K 6 (7, 7, 7, 8, 8, 8, 8) sts, PM, K to end of the row.

Short Row 6: K 6 (7, 7, 7, 7, 8, 8, 8) sts, PM, K to end of the row.

Short Rows 8 & 10: K.

Short Rows 9: K all sts working wrapped sts together with wraps.

Short Row 10: K.

Transfer all collar sts on scrap yarn.

Block

Block Back and Fronts to measurements. Sew shoulders. Transfer each shawl collar sts onto working needle and graft the ends using 3-Needle BO. Sew collar to back neckline.

Sleeves (make two)

The sleeves are worked flat first using Short Rows to shape the cap, then continued in the round from the underarm down. When convenient, switch from circular needles to DPNs before beginning to work in the rnd.

Beginning at underarm center, with RS facing K 6 (6, 6, 7, 7, 7, 8, 8) held live underarm sts, PU and K 33 (37, 40, 42, 42, 45, 48, 48) sts up to shoulder seam, PU and K 33 (37, 40, 42, 42, 45, 48, 48) sts down to live sts, K remaining 6 (6, 6, 7, 7, 7, 8, 8) live underarm sts. 78 (86, 92, 98, 98, 104, 112, 112) sts. PM's at either side of 36 center sts. Work 36 center sts following Chart 1, work the rest of sts in Rev St st.

Short Row 1 (WS): Sl 1, work in pattern to second M, SM, W&T.

Short Row 2 (RS): Work in pattern to next M, SM, W&T.

Short Row 3: Cont in pattern, working wrapped st together with wrap, remove M, W&T.

Rep Short Row 3 until there are 15 (18, 21, 23, 23, 25, 29, 28) sts left on each side of the row, ending with RS Short Row.

Next Row (WS): Work in pattern to end of the row.

Next Row (RS): Work in pattern to end of the row, removing short rows M's. PM for beginning of rnd, work remainder of Sleeve in the rnd.

Work 1 rnd in pattern, reading every Chart 1 line from right to left as a RS row.

Dec Rnd: P1, P2tog, work in pattern to last 3 sts, P2tog, P1. 2 sts dec.

Rep Dec Rnd every 8 (8, 8, 8, 8, 6, 6, 6)th rnd 9 (7, 5, 2, 5, 20, 14, 18) more times and then every 6 (6, 6, 6, 0, 4, 4)th rnd 6 (10, 13, 17, 13, 0, 9, 4) more times. 46 (50, 54, 58, 60, 62, 64, 66) sts.

Work 1 rnd in pattern, then cont to WE if necessary until length from underarm is 0.75" less than desired arm length.

Cuff

Rnd 1: K 5 (7, 9, 11, 12, 13, 14, 15), (K2tog, K2) 4 times, K2tog twice, (K2, SSK) 4 times, K 5 (7, 9, 11, 12, 13, 14, 15). 36 (40, 44, 48, 50, 52, 54, 56) sts.

Rnd 2: P.

Work even in Garter st for 5 rnds, or until Cuff measures 0.75". Loosely BO all sts.

Finishing

Weave in ends, block sleeves to measurements.

Studio Cardigan

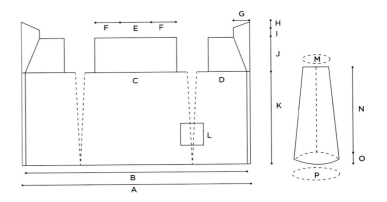

A 44 (47.25, 51.25, 53.5, 58.5, 61.5, 65.5, 72)"
B 43.25 (45.75, 50.75, 53.75, 58.25, 61.75, 66.25, 73)"
C 18.75 (20, 22.5, 24, 26.25, 28, 30.25, 33.5)"
D 10.75 (11.5, 12.5, 13.5, 14.5, 15.5, 16.5, 18.25)"
E 7 (8, 8.25, 8.5, 9, 9.25, 9.5, 10)"
F 5 (5, 6, 6.5, 7.5, 8.25, 9, 10.5)"
G 6.5 (7, 7.25, 7.5, 7.5, 7.75, 8, 8.4)"
H 1.5"
I 3.5 (4, 4.5, 4.5, 4.5, 4.75, 5, 5)"
J 7 (7.5, 8, 8.5, 8.5, 9, 9.5, 9.5)"
K 26.25"
L 5.5" before top trim
M 7 (7.75, 8.25, 9, 9.25, 9.5, 9.75, 10)"
N 18.25 (19.5, 19.75, 19.75, 19.75, 19.75, 19.75, 20.5)"
O 1.75 (2, 2, 2.25, 2.25, 2.5, 2.5, 3)"
P 12 (13.25, 14, 15, 15, 16, 17.25, 17.25)"

Gauge Chart

Legend:

□ **knit**
RS: knit stitch
WS: purl stitch

⊡ **purl**
RS: purl stitch
WS: knit stitch

▨ **garter ST (all sizes)**
knit stitches

■ **stockinette ST (larger sizes)**
RS: knit stitch
WS: purl stitch

▭ **pattern repeat**

— **smaller chart ends**

c2 over 1 right P
SL1 to CN, hold in back.
K2, P1 from CN

c2 over 1 left P
SL2 to CN, hold in front.
P1, K2 from CN

c2 over 2 right
SL2 to CN, hold in back.
K2, K2 from CN

c2 over 2 left
SL2 to CN, hold in front.
K2, K2 from CN

Chart 1

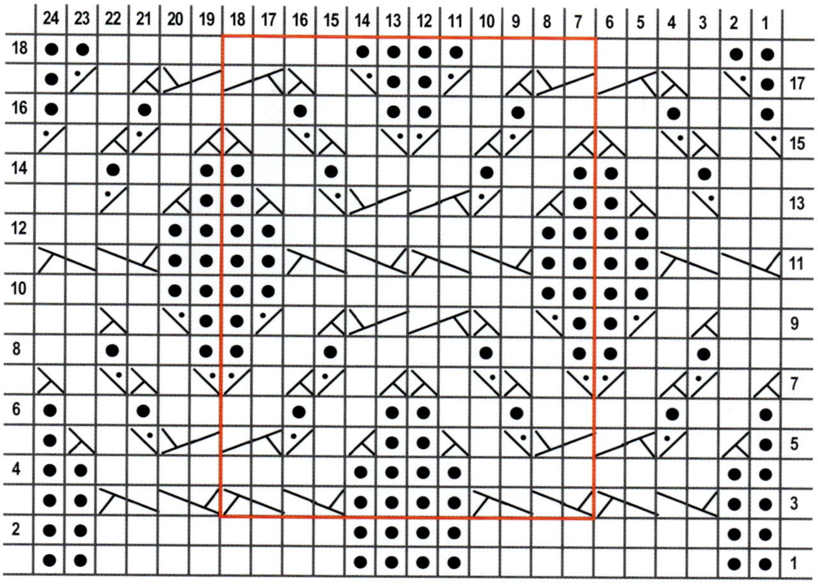

Chart 2

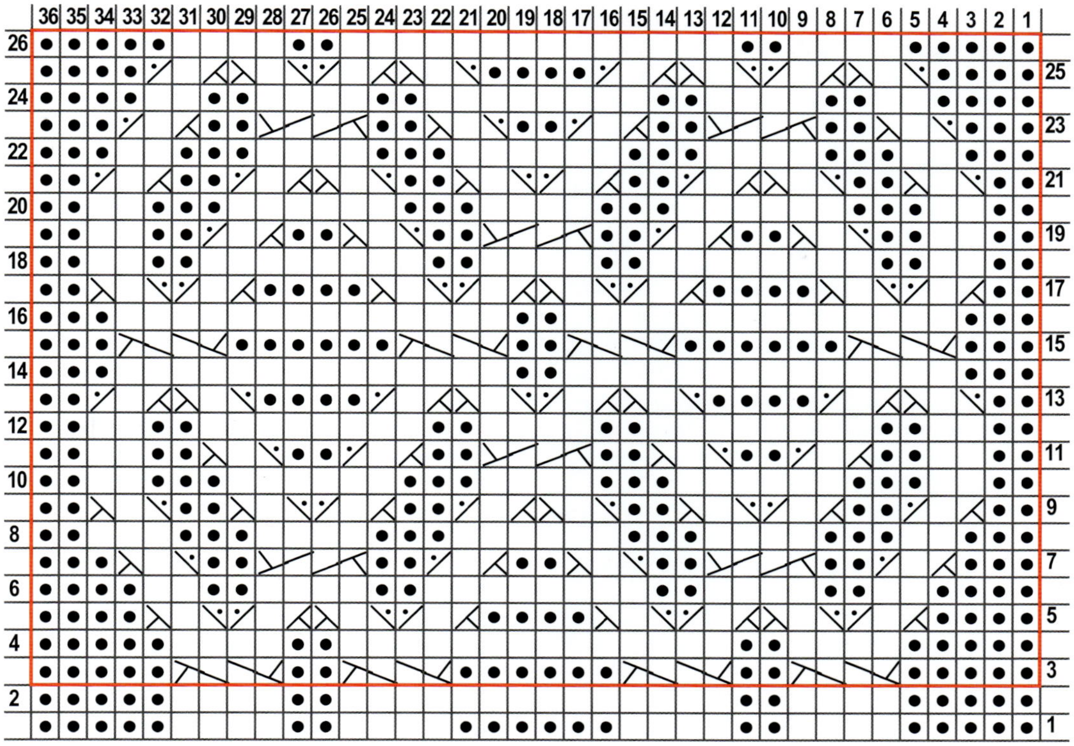

Studio Cardigan 117

Chart 3: size 40.25-42.75

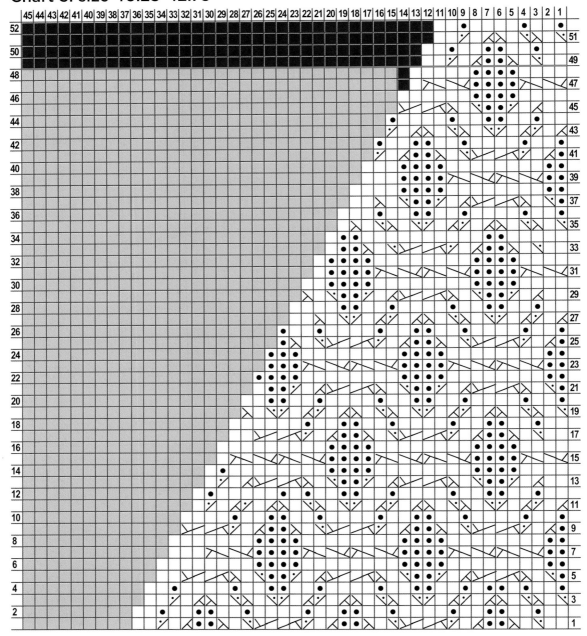

Chart 3: size 47.75

Studio Cardigan 119

Chart 3: size 50.75-55.25

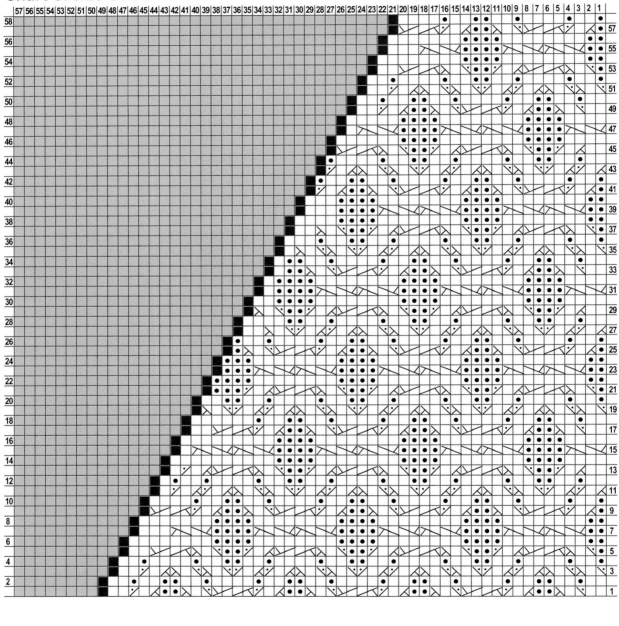

Chart 3: size 58.75

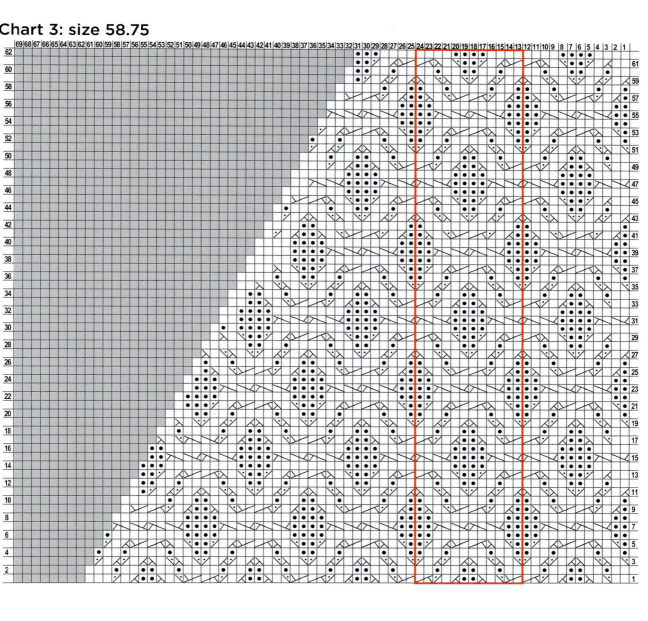

Studio Cardigan 121

Chart 3: size 63.25-69.75

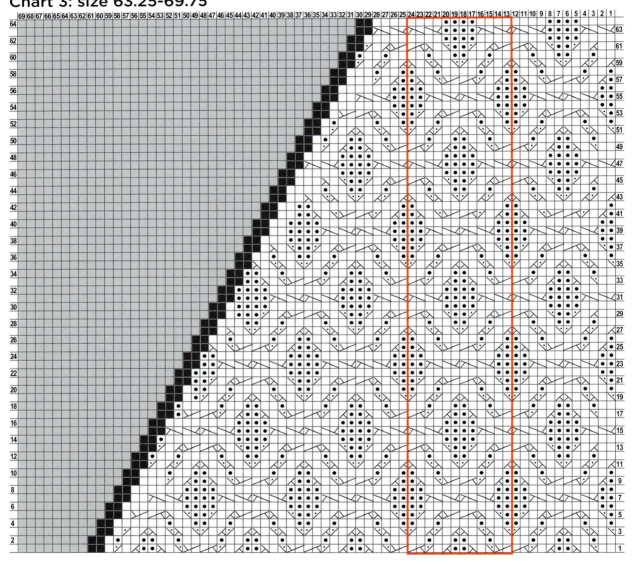

122 Studio Cardigan

Chart 4: size 40.25-42.75

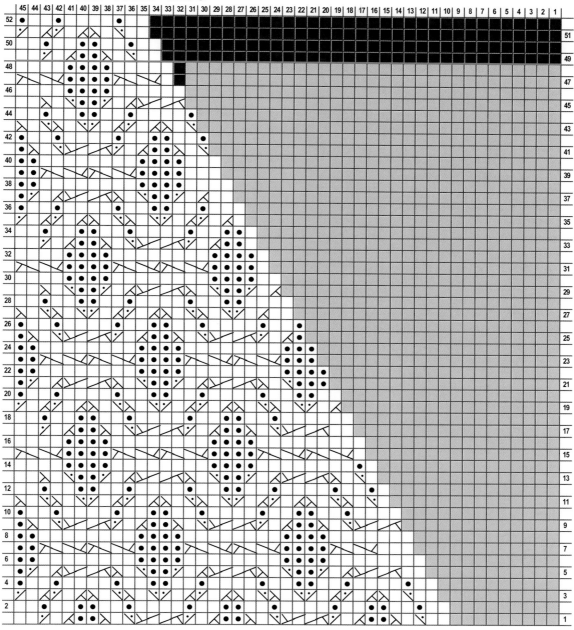

Studio Cardigan

Chart 4: size 47.75

Chart 4: size 50.745-55.25

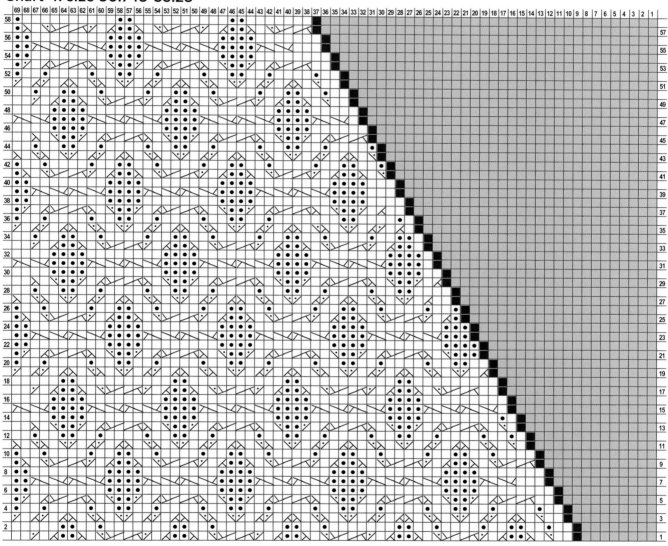

Studio Cardigan 125

Chart 4: size 58.75

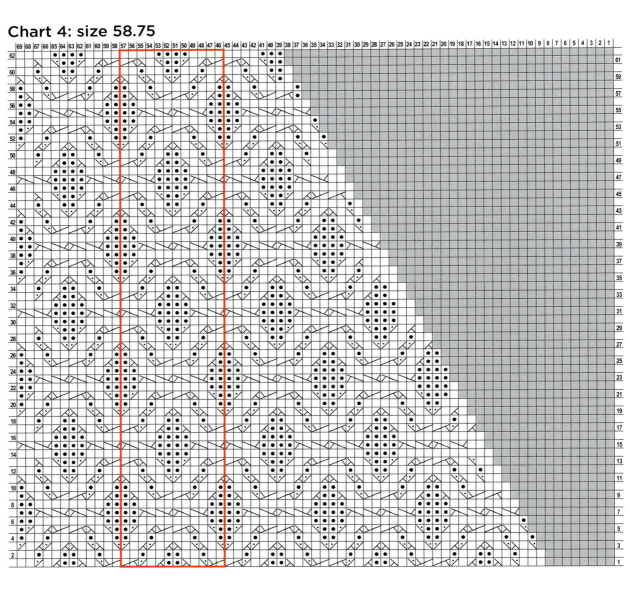

126 Studio Cardigan

Chart 4: size 63.25-69.75

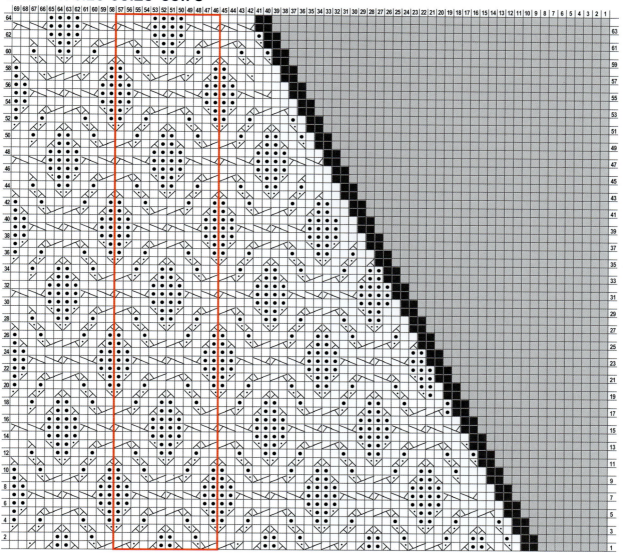

Studio Cardigan 127

PINEY TWEED HAT

by Emily Kintigh

FINISHED MEASUREMENTS
19.5 (21, 22.5, 24)" circumference x 6.75 (8, 9.25, 10.5)" high

YARN
Knit Picks Stroll Tweed (65% Superwash Merino Wool, 25% Nylon, 10% Donegal; 123 yards/50g): Forest Heather 26298, 1 (1, 2, 2) balls

NEEDLES
US 1 (2.25mm) 16" circular needles, or two sizes less than needle to obtain gauge

US 3 (3.25mm) 16" circular needles and DPNs, or two 24" circular needles for two circulars technique, or one 32" or longer circular needle for Magic Loop technique, or size to obtain gauge

NOTIONS
Yarn Needle, Stitch Markers, Cable Needle

GAUGE
32 sts and 40 rnds = 4" over Piney Tweed Chart in the rnd on larger needles, blocked

For pattern support, contact auntieemsstudio@gmail.com

Piney Tweed Hat

Notes:

The chart for the hat has two cable panels which form the same cable, but are offset so that while one is wide, the next one is thin. The chart is repeated three times around the hat for a total of six cable panels and six moss stitch sections. Read each row from right to left.

When placing the markers, it is helpful to use different markers at the end of an entire chart repeat from those indicating repeats within the chart.

The size measurements are for the finished hat circumference. The hat will stretch a bit to fit slightly larger head circumferences.

2x2 Ribbing (in the rnd over a multiple of 4 sts)
Rnd 1: (K2, P2) to end.
Rep Rnd 1 for pattern.

DIRECTIONS

Brim

With smaller needles, loosely CO 156 (168, 180, 192) sts. PM and join in the rnd being careful not to twist the sts. Work in 2x2 Ribbing until piece measures 1.25 (1.5, 1.75, 2)" from CO edge.

Main Hat

Switch to larger needles.

Begin working from Piney Tweed Chart beginning with Rnd 1 (11, 1, 11) of chart. Place markers as follows on the first rnd worked: *Rep sts 1-2 of chart over the first 10 (12, 14, 16) sts of the rnd, PM, work sts 3-18 of the chart, PM, rep sts 19-20 over the next 10 (12, 14, 16) sts of the rnd, PM, work sts 21-36 of the chart, PM; rep from * two more times. The chart is repeated three times across the rnd.

Continue working as indicated below, repeating chart sts 1-2 over the 10 (12, 14, 16) sts between the beginning of the rnd and the first marker, working sts 3-18 of chart over the sts between the first and second markers, sts 19-20 over the 10 (12, 14, 16) sts between the second and third markers, and sts 21-36 over the sts between the third and fourth markers, and repeating this pattern twice more across the rnd.

Note: When working the Crown Decreases Chart, the markers are not necessary, but are helpful for keeping track of where you are. Remove the markers when they are no longer needed or helpful. Switch to DPNs when sts no longer fit comfortably on circular needle.

For 19.5" size: Work Rnds 2-20 of Piney Tweed Chart, then Rnds 1-4, then move on to Crown Decreases Chart starting on Rnd 13 and working through end of chart. Cut yarn and pull through remaining sts.

For 21" size: Work Rnds 12-20 of Piney Tweed Chart, then Rnds 1-20, then move on to Crown Decreases Chart starting on Rnd 9 and working through end of chart. Cut yarn and pull through remaining sts.

For 22.5" size: Work Rnds 2-20 of Piney Tweed Chart, then Rnds 1-16, then move on to Crown Decreases Chart starting on Rnd 5 and working through end of chart. Cut yarn and pull through remaining sts.

For 24" size: Work Rnds 12-20 of Piney Tweed Chart, then Rnds 1-20, then Rnds 1- 12, then move on to Crown Decreases Chart starting on Rnd 1 and working through end of chart. Cut yarn and pull through remaining sts.

Finishing

Weave in ends, wash and block.

Piney Tweed Chart

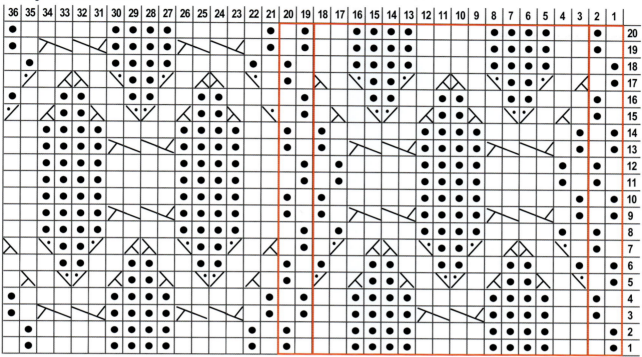

Legend:

- ⊡ **purl** — purl stitch
- ☐ **knit** — knit stitch
- ◿ **k2tog** — knit two stitches together as one stitch
- ◺ **SSK** — Slip one stitch as if to knit, Slip another stitch as if to knit. Insert left-hand needle into front of these 2 stitches and knit them together
- ◿ **P2TOG** — Purl 2 stitches together
- ◿ **P3TOG** — Purl three stitches together as one
- ▓ **no stitch**

- **C2 over 1 left P** — SL2 STS onto CN, hold in front, P1, K2 from CN
- **C2 over 1 right P** — SL1 ST onto CN, hold in back, K2, P1 from CN
- **C4F** — SL2 STS onto CN, hold in front K2, K2 from CN
- ☐ **pattern repeat** (orange)
- ☐ **marker** (blue)

Piney Tweed Hat   131

Crown Decreases Chart

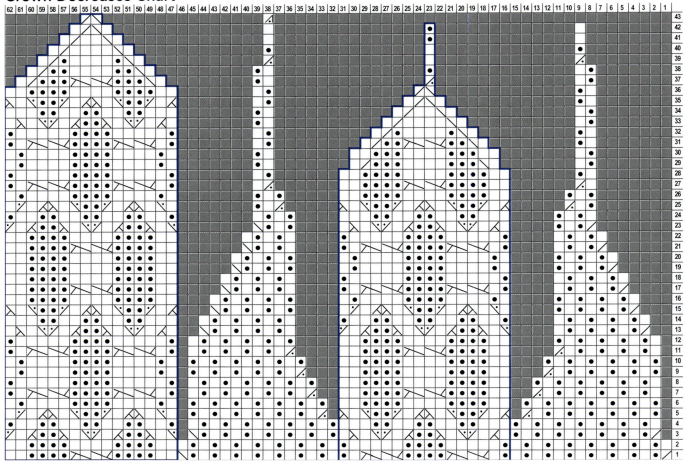

Abbreviations		**K-wise**	knitwise	**rep**	repeat		tog
BO	bind off	**LH**	left hand	**Rev St st**	reverse stockinette stitch	**St st**	stockinette stitch
cn	cable needle	**M**	marker			**sts**	stitch(es)
CC	contrast color	**M1**	make one stitch	**RH**	right hand	**TBL**	through back loop
CDD	Centered double dec	**M1L**	make one left-leaning stitch	**rnd(s)**	round(s)	**TFL**	through front loop
				RS	right side	**tog**	together
CO	cast on	**M1R**	make one right-leaning stitch	**Sk**	skip	**W&T**	wrap & turn (see specific instructions in pattern)
cont	continue			**Sk2p**	sl 1, k2tog, pass slipped stitch over k2tog: 2 sts dec		
dec	decrease(es)	**MC**	main color				
DPN(s)	double pointed needle(s)	**P**	purl			**WE**	work even
		P2tog	purl 2 sts together	**SKP**	sl, k, psso: 1 st dec	**WS**	wrong side
EOR	every other row	**PM**	place marker	**SL**	slip	**WYIB**	with yarn in back
inc	increase	**PFB**	purl into the front and back of stitch	**SM**	slip marker	**WYIF**	with yarn in front
K	knit			**SSK**	sl, sl, k these 2 sts tog	**YO**	yarn over
K2tog	knit two sts together	**PSSO**	pass slipped stitch over	**SSP**	sl, sl, p these 2 sts tog tbl		
KFB	knit into the front and back of stitch	**PU**	pick up	**SSSK**	sl, sl, sl, k these 3 sts		
		P-wise	purlwise				

Knit Picks yarn is both luxe and affordable—a seeming contradiction trounced! But it's not just about the pretty colors; we also care deeply about fiber quality and fair labor practices, leaving you with a gorgeously reliable product you'll turn to time and time again.

THIS COLLECTION FEATURES

Palette
Fingering Weight
100% Peruvian Highland Wool

Andean Treasure
Sport Weight
100% Baby Alpaca

Hawthorne Tonal
Fingering Weight
80% Superwash Fine Highland Wool, 20% Polyamide (Nylon)

Swish
Worsted Weight
100% Superwash Merino Wool

Stroll Tweed
Fingering Weight
65% Superwash Merino Wool, 25% Nylon, 10% Donegal

Wool of the Andes Tweed
Worsted Weight
80% Peruvian Highland Wool, 20% Donegal Tweed

Wool of the Andes
Worsted Weight & Sport Weight
100% Peruvian Highland Wool

Wool of the Andes Superwash
Worsted Weight
100% Superwash Wool

Wool of the Andes
Bulky Weight
100% Peruvian Highland Wool

View these beautiful yarns and more at www.KnitPicks.com